TONI SAVORY

Mastering the
TAROT
TABLEAU

*Revisiting Predictive Accuracy
with Tarot*

REDFeather™
MIND | BODY | SPIRIT

Designed by BMac
Type set in Minion/Bodoni

ISBN: 978-0-7643-6891-2
ePub: 978-1-5073-0558-4
Printed in India

FSC
www.fsc.org
MIX
Paper | Supporting responsible forestry
FSC® C016779

Published by REDFeather Mind, Body, Spirit
An imprint of Schiffer Publishing, Ltd.
4880 Lower Valley Road
Atglen, PA 19310
Phone: (610) 593-1777; Fax: (610) 593-2002
Email: Info@redfeathermbs.com
Web: www.redfeathermbs.com

For our complete selection of fine books on this and related subjects, please visit our website at www.schifferbooks.com. You may also write for a free catalog.

REDFeather Mind, Body, Spirit's titles are available at special discounts for bulk purchases for sales promotions or premiums. Special editions, including personalized covers, corporate imprints, and excerpts, can be created in large quantities for special needs. For more information, contact the publisher.

We are always looking for people to write books on new and related subjects. If you have an idea for a book, please contact us at proposals@schifferbooks.com.

"

Mastering the Tarot Tableau is an illuminating book that reveals how every card and every reading tells a story. It offers a treasure trove of insights into our relationships and fortunes. With the innovative tableau spreads, readers will learn from a great teacher and will be empowered to harness the Tarot's narrative to illuminate their path. Dive in and discover the art of prediction—it's about the game of life, a journey you won't want to miss!

"

Amy Zerner & Monte Farber, authors of the
Zerner-Farber Tarot and the *Enchanted Love Tarot*

"

What sets Toni Savory's Mastering the Tarot Tableau apart from the many popular Tarot books that came before is its laser focus on practical, applicable strategies for enhancing predictive accuracy. Savory's expertise shines through in the power-packed techniques that will wow even the seasoned reader. This is one of the most useful and comprehensive guides to Tarot reading I've encountered.

"

Benebell Wen, authors of *Holistic Tarot*

"

At last, the ultimate method of reading Tarot through the techniques of classic cartomancy is revealed by Toni Savory! These precise reading methods provide templates of revelation for every Tarot reader —when you use the maps provided, you will never need to guess or wonder what cards mean, because you will see for yourself.

"

Caitlín Matthews, author of *Time-Changer's Tarot* and *Untold Tarot*

"

Toni is one of the rare authors who truly possesses knowledge and proficiency in many modalities. Once again, she shares her wisdom with us in a groundbreaking yet approachable Tarot book. Learn to read Tarot or level up your practice with this latest Savory treasure.

"

Michelle Welch, author of *The Magic of Connection, Spirits Unveiled,* and *A Psychic's Handbook*

"

This book offers a fresh perspective on using Tarot cards with the Lenormand system's structured, no-nonsense spreads and methods, allowing for accurate readings and depth to your divination. Toni brings her love of both systems to this deck, and if you're ready to explore Tarot's richness with Lenormand's clarity, this is the must-have book for your collection.

"

Ethony Dawn, author of *Tarot Grimoire*

This book would not have been possible without the unwavering support and encouragement of my amazing partner, Jane. Not only have you been my rock, but you have also dedicated your time to make sure my words make sense! Thank you from the bottom of my heart for every moment. A dedication wouldn't be complete without Lloyd and Nate, the most incredibly understanding, helpful, and of course energetic boys who share their view of the world with me from a kid's perspective. A little of that insight is within the pages of everything I write. I am grateful to every member of the World Divination Association—you have colored the pages of this book with every comment or words of support throughout the years.

To the REDFeather imprint of Schiffer Publishing, a heartfelt thank-you for your continued support in my divination journey. Chris and Peggy in particular, you were nothing short of amazing in incorporating my words into the book you read today.

Introduction

Mastering the Tarot Tableau: Revisiting Predictive Accuracy with Tarot has been created to enrich the Tarot reader's interpretations with predictive accuracy. Although the tableau style is not commonly read in the English-speaking Tarot world, it is the go-to method for many readers in Europe who prefer the storytelling narrative of the tableau over a restrictive placement spread. Each Tarot deck contains the story of life, and every possible situation is available for insight. By using a tableau spread, we can determine interpersonal relationships and auspicious versus inauspicious fortunes and tell the tale of daily life for our querents.

The Tarot tableau narrative-style reading techniques found within the pages of this book are used throughout Europe and have been passed down through generations of readers. Many techniques have been developed through the use of systems as games of chance, such as the Game of Hope, Lenormand, or the Skat System of "patience" tableau. History and location of the reader greatly determine their style of tableau. For example, nineteenth-century fortune-tellers in Bavaria found their favorite systems of divination to be outlawed, making way for the diviner to become creative with their divination practice. Divination systems such as Kipperkarten and Lenormand were brought to fruition (due to their pictorial offerings, which could be covertly read whilst seemingly playing a "game of chance"), and "patience games"—like the card game known as "solitaire" in the USA—were played in lieu of a spread. Diviners did not wish to be seen divining and therefore had to portray themselves as entertainers or simply persons playing a game of patience, whilst secretly reading their client's fortune. Many formats of tableau were used to "hide" their fortune-telling activities, together with "fans" of cards held by both the diviner and the client. The techniques you will be employing in your tableau readings are using the "game play" of a system, which has garnered techniques from multiple systems including Tarot de Marseille, Playing-Card Cartomancy,

Lenormand, Kipper cards, Gypsy cards, Skat, Königsrufen, and Le Grand Jeu Lenormand, which use common principles of directional cues and house system techniques.

The tableau provides the backdrop for a pure predictive reading, quite like the fortune-tellers of the nineteenth century would employ, leaving spiritual matters to the side and focusing on what will happen within the daily life of a client. All flowery language attached to the Tarot meanings are removed for a short, sharp, and direct narrative. The tableau is interpreted in a conversational manner with the storyline building at every step, allowing the reader the freedom to flow through the tableau, substantiating their narrative with every card added.

The reader finds that their readings become a novel-like affair, and the story of the querent's life is explained from start to finish with flair.

WHAT IS A GRAND TABLEAU?

The name "Grand Tableau" comes from the French "Le Grand Tableau" and the German "die Große Tafel" (which translates to "large board") and refers to laying out the cards in one of the following traditional layouts:

The Standard Tableau, 8 × 4

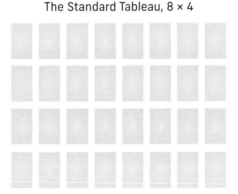

The Grand Tableau, 8 × 4 + 4

The German Tableau, 9 × 4

The Game of Hope, 6 × 6

The Tarot Tableau, 9 × 8 + 6

A tableau is a snapshot of the future, showing interpersonal relationships, situations, advice, and motivations all clear for the reader to extract. Consider the planning stages of a movie or book narrative: the main characters are described, scenes are created, and a narrative/dialogue is formed. Each frame of a movie or chapter of a book has a number of scenes that tie together into a final depiction of the scene in question. Apply this idea to cards explaining the scene, and you can see that the tableau is a visual representation of the querent's life in the set time period. Each action, influence, and behavior will be highlighted in the picture you have laid out, including a full description of their state of being.

A tableau is based on the game play of your system of choice. That is to say, with a Tarot deck, you could complete all tableaus listed, but with a thirty-two- or thirty-six-card system, the reader may choose the smaller variants that fit the number of cards being used. The placements within the tableau are based on the cards being laid out in numerical order (for example, 1 through 36 for the 8 × 4 + 4 placement), with each placement explaining the status of the card landing within (see the section "The Houses").

The Tarot Suits Tableau, 10 × 4

The Nine-Card Tableau

However, in order to lay a tableau, we need to ensure only that at least one card has all dynamic placements; that is to say, that one card can be fully surrounded with cards above, below, and side to side (*see image on p. 14*). Therefore, a tableau can consist of nine cards.

The Nine-Card Tableau is the perfect starting point to gain confidence in reading the larger spreads. It can be used for clarity in any situation and will increase the understanding of the dynamics within your Tarot deck, building confidence in directionality as well as exploring the auspicious versus inauspicious tableau techniques.

The tableau spreads explored within the pages of this book will offer the reader many layers of interpretation and techniques to extract clear predictions for your querent, highlighting the true versatility of Tarot and how it has never been nor ever will be a one-trick pony.

HOW TO USE THIS BOOK

Whether you are a seasoned reader or brand new to Tarot, you will find techniques within this book to enhance your predictive accuracy. You may use any number of the techniques provided to conduct your reading. Simply choose a section to begin, then lay out your cards! Please note that the "Meanings" section of this book includes important information about directionality, movement, and amplification, along with each card's core essence.

The Game of Tarot	Tarot deck fundamentals
The Meanings	Core meanings plus card directionality, movement, and more
Tarot Tableau Basics	Everything you need to know to start reading a tableau.
Advanced Tarot Techniques	The extra steps in a tableau to build narrative
Quick Glance	All the keywords and important information in table format
Client Readings	A full Tarot Tableau example

The Game of Tarot

THE GAME OF TAROT MEANINGS

Thinking of your Tarot tableau as a game to be played is the perfect mindset for imaginative and intuitive readings. Consider a board game: we throw the dice and move along the rows of the board until we finally either win or lose. Each position on the board has a rule (e.g., receive five gold pieces), and we have to overcome a few obstacles along the way. The game of Tarot is no different—we follow the flow of the board to interpret a narrative, using each card as a further step in the story of life. The Game of Hope is one of the most well-known board games with a divination deck and teaches us the importance of following the cards through their placements to the culmination of the interpretation in the winning "house." How the cards fall within this backdrop of a board game explains how close to a perfect life your querent will experience. That is to say, if all cards fell in order (i.e., sequentially correct from start to finish), then the querent is living the most successful and fulfilling life possible. Every deviation from this sequence highlights the intricacies of real-life situations, whereby each moment in life creates the next in a butterfly effect.

A tableau reading is traditionally a no-nonsense, predictively accurate approach where the reader focuses on life events and their manifestation in the querent's life. Therefore, the keywords for your Tarot deck should remain within the realm of everyday occurrences and life themes. Naturally, should you wish to provide spiritual advice for a client, more-esoteric vocabulary can be used; however, the tableau-style reading should maintain a succinct, practical, and no-fluff approach. The most important piece of advice in interpreting a tableau is to remember that you are no longer reading single cards! Each card is influenced by at least three others, and their meanings combine into a cohesive storyline that offers a deeper narrative. This approach builds confidence in every reader, whether novice or professional.

The meanings in this book represent the fundamental core meanings of each card in everyday life. It is important to note the core keywords and develop your own vocabulary to interpret them. For example, a keyword for the Two of Swords is "decisions"; consider the surrounding cards to determine the nature of these "decisions" in relation to the question posed.

TAROT FUNDAMENTALS

The Tarot deck consists of seventy-eight cards.

The deck is split into two "ARCANA"—two magical parts.

The **Major Arcana** consists of twenty-two cards. The "major cards" of the deck depict significant life events or "happenings." These twenty-two cards are rather "grand" in their nature and, as such, provide a larger-scale reading, highlighting major life events.

The **Minor Arcana** is made up of fifty-six cards divided into four suits. These are your daily happenings, the mundane details we encounter. When explaining a story, you always have a majority of details with fewer of "full-scale" events.

Imagine sitting down with a director who explains the storyboard of a new Marvel adventure (choose any story genre that suits). Now, consider what actually happens in the movie. There will be extensive scene setting and probably many people sitting around tables discussing or walking through town with dialogue. These represent the Minor Arcana situations, the nitty-gritty details that lay out the story for you. Then, the action unfolds on a cosmic scale, altering the entire world as a result. . . . Welcome to Major Arcana—the significant seismic happenings.

Within the Minor Arcana, we also have the **Court cards** (you will recognize them from your playing-card decks). These are the "people cards" within the deck, representing individuals who embody the characteristics of their respective suits.

THE SIGNIFICATOR CARD

The card that performs the center of your interpretation in the tableau is the "significator" for your querent. The entire reading revolves around where the significator is placed and whether the situation depicted demands an auspicious (positive) or inauspicious (negative) interpretation. Before each session, you will choose a King or Queen to perform the role of significator, and all other cards in the tableau will be read in accordance with their placement in relation to the significator.

The significator card will also determine the direction of the narrative:

Right-facing significator   read from left to right

Left-facing significator   read from right to left

NOTE: Reversals are not used in tableau readings, since the tableau will clearly show the reader how to determine a negative versus positive aspect of the cards on the basis of their placement.

Auspicious cards are those placed ahead of the King or Queen in the tableau. These placements highlight situations in the querent's life that will be easily managed within the set time frame. When negative cards appear in this area, it indicates challenges that the querent will confront directly, retaining control over the situation.

RIGHT FACING

Inauspicious   Auspicious

LEFT FACING

Auspicious   Inauspicious

Inauspicious cards are those that are positioned behind the King or Queen in the tableau, highlighting difficulties within the querent's life. This suggests they may lack the desired control and will find these situations more difficult to manage.

The "Meanings" section contains keywords both for auspicious and inauspicious placements. Note that the inauspicious meaning for each card is based on its core meaning in that position, not from being reversed.

PICTORIAL CUES

The famous Rider-Waite Tarot deck is graced with directional cues within the cards that are used to create a fluid tableau narrative. The card meanings throughout this book are based on the directional cues found in the Rider-Waite-Smith deck. If the artwork of your chosen deck differs, be ready to utilize the imagery on each card in the deck you are using to determine the directional cues for your reading. For example, should your deck have a directional cue that differs, you will employ the directions on the artwork in your own deck. Not all cards will have a directional cue. The World, for example, does not show any movement out of the card.

Types of Cards within the Tarot Deck:

The Significator	The card to represent your querent (King or Queen only)
Directional	The imagery clearly faces left or right (e.g., Queen of Swords).
Movement	A flow of movement in the imagery (e.g., 8 of Cups)
Highlight	The imagery "points" or "signals" to another card around (e.g., the Magician)
Stationary	The image is static with no directional cues.

DIRECTIONAL CARDS

The figure in a directional card clearly faces left or right. The Court cards form the majority of the directional cards, with many Major Arcana also associated with a backward or forward motion.

Examples:

The Fool card in the Rider-Waite deck faces to the left. The card ahead of the Fool (card 1) shows the destination of that adventure or the action that will first be taken in this leap of faith. The card behind the Fool's back (card 3) shows the motivation for the adventure.

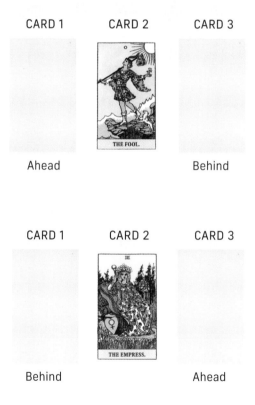

The Empress card, however, faces right. The card behind her back (card 1) highlights the motivation for the nurturing situation, whereas the card ahead of the Empress (card 3) shows what is being nurtured or the next action of nurturing.

Rule of Thumb:

Cards ahead of a directional cue (*see above*) explain the next actions in this situation.

Cards behind a directional cue (*see above*) explain the motivations for this situation.

MOVEMENT CARDS

The movement cards within the Tarot deck highlight the directions in which we form our narrative and build upon the querent's story. Take a moment to look through your favorite Tarot deck and notice any movements you may see.

Example 1

CARD 1   CARD 2   CARD 3

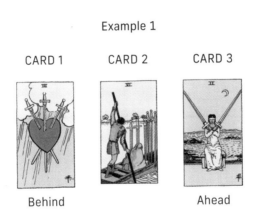

Behind   Ahead

Rule-of-Thumb Movement Cards

Movement cards with directional cues that flow with the direction of narration show movement into the future.

Movement cards with directional cues that flow against the direction of narration indicate a return to a previous situation (a move backward).

Example 1: Horizontal Movement

The movement depicted in the Six of Swords clearly marks a route toward the right-hand side of the card. In the example above, the Six of Swords is moving away from the heartache of the Three of Swords and moving toward the tough decisions of the Two of Swords. This highlights that the querent will be making difficult decisions once they decide to move beyond the heartache currently felt.

EXAMPLE 1 (ALTERNATE VERSION)

Ahead   Behind

In an alternative position, the Six of Swords heads directly into heartbreak, confirming that any decisions made will lead to heartbreak.

Example 2: Vertical Movement

CARD ABOVE   Seven of Wands

CARD BELOW   Three of Pentacles

In the Seven of Wands, we can see that the figure is defending himself against the people beneath him. If you look to the card below, you will understand what he is defending himself against. In this example, the querent is defending themselves against their coworkers or the collaborative work itself!

Example 2   Example 3

HIGHLIGHT CARDS

Highlight cards provide a little additional cue to check one (or several) of the surrounding cards. The core meaning of the highlight card will explain the situation into which the surrounding cards are drawn.

Example 3:

The Hanged Man is upside down in his frame, highlighting the card below. Look to the card beneath the Hanged Man to understand what should be put on hold, or what situation needs another perspective.

Example 4:

The Magician directs attention to the cards positioned top left and bottom right (indicated by his gesturing arms). These two cards explain what skills are required or what the querent needs to manipulate to manifest the best situation. In the example below, the Eight of Pentacles and Four of Pentacles show that the querent should focus on honing their workplace skills and keeping their current position.

Example 4

STATIONARY CARDS

The stationary cards provide a welcome break from the movement in the above cards. They can punctuate the situations unfolding within the tableau in an interpretation or can be used as a significator card, which is then highlighted, with the surrounding cards leading the interpretation and providing a further description and narrative.

TIPS FOR READING A TABLEAU

The most important thing to remember is that you are reading all cards and their interactions as one narrative. In the instructions for earlier card games, we find a simple piece of "fortune-telling advice" suggesting to "create a fun and entertaining narrative beginning with our significator." A tableau reading should be enjoyable; being too rigid about techniques in the beginning may stunt your flow a little. Try incorporating one technique at a time to see which enables you to have the most fluid narrative—and stick to it!

The term "bop around the board" is a perfect example of a fluid reading style, encouraging the reader to begin with the significator and then pick out cards above, below, ahead, and behind before jumping into further narrative. By approaching the reading one step at a time, you will soon be regaling your friends with fluid and flowing interpretation.

Finally, imagine you were making a bowl of soup. Many ingredients are needed to get the perfect balance of herbs and substance—a little too much of one ingredient will spoil the entire pot. The Tarot tableau is no different. Every card represents an ingredient in the querent's life within the specified time frame. Imagine you were to put all the cards presenting into a blender. What flavor would they present to you? Would they be salty (with a lot of negative cards present)? Or sweet (with many positives)? The presence of many Major Arcana cards heightens the severity of the reading, indicating significant life events, while lots of Court cards highlight interpersonal relationships. View the cards in a tableau as a cohesive whole; each card contributes to the overall narrative.

THE FOOL.

THE MAGICIAN.

THE HIGH PRIESTESS.

THE EMPRESS.

THE EMPEROR.

THE HIEROPHANT.

THE LOVERS.

THE CHARIOT.

STRENGTH.

THE HERMIT.

WHEEL of FORTUNE.

JUSTICE.

THE HANGED MAN.

DEATH.

TEMPERANCE.

THE DEVIL.

THE TOWER.

THE STAR.

THE MOON.

THE SUN.

JUDGEMENT.

THE WORLD.

The Meanings

THE MAJOR ARCANA

The Major Arcana cards (cards 0–XXI) signify major life events and appear in a tableau when the importance of a situation needs to be raised. A tableau with few Majors suggests a run-of-the-mill year without major life events, while a tableau filled with Majors indicates a year marked by significant life events related to the theme of the reading (e.g., marriage, health, loss, divorce, pregnancy). The Majors play an integral role in explaining the significance of the reading, and, of course, their core meanings add important advice in any situation.

The Major Arcana is a life's work to understand and work through. If we spent all year on these twenty-two cards, we would certainly still find new nuances to learn! However, when working with dynamics and tableau placements, it is wise to begin with the core essence of the Major attending in order to form a narrative with the surrounding cards.

Consider the Major Arcana as the game of life: we experience the highlights, lowlights, and every rollercoaster in between. Every Major that is added to the spread increases the significance of the year ahead. That is to say, each Major amplifies a situation in the querent's life, making it more significant—the more Majors, the larger the life event shown. In each of the card meanings below, you will find details on how each Major can raise the significance of a situation.

0. Fool

Auspicious   Folly, spontaneity, unconventional, innocence

Inauspicious Impulsive, rash, folly

The Fool inspires us to step out of our comfort zone and embark on a new adventure. In a positive placement, he embodies the most-exciting first steps we can take; in a negative placement, he becomes hasty, sporadic, and dangerously naive.

Direction   The Fool faces away from the rest of the Major Arcana, in a world of his own. The card behind The Fool's back shows where the querent is leaping from (or the motivation behind the spontaneity), and the card ahead of the Fool will show where this journey is heading.

Amplifies   A leap of faith or quickens the pace

I. Magician

Auspicious   Skill, powers, self-confidence, resourcefulness, conscious power

Inauspicious Manipulation, trickery, untapped talents

The Magician teaches us to believe in our own abilities and know that we possess the necessary skills for the situation. In a positive placement, the Magician urges us to take action and be confident; in a negative placement, he becomes manipulative and speaks of our inability to commit to our skills.

Direction   The Magician is a highlighter card. He holds his hands and highlights the cards diagonally (above left and bottom right). The two highlighted cards can be combined to understand what skill mix is required (or what manipulation is at play in a negative placement).

Amplifies   Effortlessness and extra skill sets

II. High Priestess

Auspicious   Intuition, ethereal wisdom, mystery, secrets

Inauspicious   Secrets, not listening to intuition

The High Priestess card attends when we need to follow our intuition. The cards surrounding the High Priestess will confirm what aspects of the situation need a deeper look. Positively placed, the High Priestess emphasizes the need to seek the answers within rather than pursue external advice. However, in a negative placement, check the surrounding cards to understand what secrets have not been revealed or which situation is not on the querent's radar.

Direction   Stationary

Amplifies   Awareness or the need to be intuitive

III. Empress

Auspicious   Nurture, nature, fertility, abundance

Inauspicious   Nonnurturing, overbearing, lack of growth

The Empress radiates with femininity and abundance; she will protect and nurture a situation from conception through to completion. In a positive placement, the Empress enhances all the surrounding cards, sharing her motherly nature and cultivating growth. When negatively placed, the Empress becomes less nurturing, leaving the surrounding cards wanting for more attention.

Direction   The Empress faces right; the card behind her back reveals what led to this situation, while the card ahead explains what situation is being nurtured (or needs to be nurtured) the most.

Amplifies   Growth and active acceptance

IV. Emperor

Auspicious   Authority, power, protection, leadership

Inauspicious   Inflexible, domineering, excessive control

The Emperor exudes masculinity and power. He will enforce rules and lead the way forward with authority and control. Positively placed, the Emperor can represent any figurehead in the querent's life and situations involving external authority. In a negative position, the Emperor highlights situations where excessive control is an aspect or where an authority figure has a negative impact on the querent's life.

Direction   Stationary

Amplifies   Control, both positively and negatively

V. The Hierophant

Auspicious   Religion, tradition, education, convention

Inauspicious   Dogmatic, overly structured, following blindly

The Hierophant is our spiritual code of ethics in one card. As a spiritual leader, he embodies the doctrine associated with his belief systems with both authority and spiritual wisdom. In a tableau, the Hierophant can represent any established tradition and its principles or can indicate a need to structure our belief systems. In a positive placement, the Hierophant speaks of good associations with the surrounding cards. Negatively placed, the Hierophant becomes dogmatic and structured to the point of being unhealthful or indicates that we are blindly following a structure without any analysis.

Direction   Stationary

Amplifies   Structure, both positively and negatively

VI. Lovers

Auspicious   Love, connection, relationship, choice

Inauspicious   Disharmony, relationship issues

The Lovers card highlights our connections and relationships. In a positive aspect, the Lovers speak of pure connection and a solid relationship. However, when the Lovers is placed behind the back of our Querent or Partner card (Court card), it showcases everything that is wrong in our relationships. The cards around the Lovers card explain what is happening within our interpersonal connections, with the cards on the left and right solidified within the partnership.

Direction	Highlight. The Lovers card highlights the cards on the left and right (with the two people in the imagery) and pulls them into a partnership.
Amplifies	Connection and relationships

VII. The Chariot

Auspicious	Overcoming obstacles, taking control, confidence
Inauspicious	Lack of drive, lack of direction

The Chariot is a card full of momentum and forward drive. It can show the confidence we have or the drive we possess to complete our goals. When the Chariot sits ahead of the Querent or Partner card, it speaks of positive momentum within the querent's life. However, in a negative aspect, it shows that the necessary drive is lacking or the querent is unsure where to focus their abilities. The cards on the left and right of the Chariot will explain its movement.

Direction	Highlight. The two sphinxes draw the cards on the left and right into the movement of the Chariot.
Amplifies	Movement and drive

VIII. Strength

Auspicious	Strength, courage, fearlessness, fortitude
Inauspicious	Assertion, opposing force, forcefulness

The Strength card adds power into the situation (for better or worse!). When in a positive placement ahead of the significator, Strength speaks of fortitude, determination, and courage—the strength required to move forward and gain advantage in any given situation. Placed behind the significator, Strength becomes a negative influence and morphs into aggressive behavior, forcefulness, and forces that work against us.

Direction	Directional cue—left. The card to the left of Strength shows what is needing fortitude. The card to the right of Strength shows what situation is motivating this.
Amplifies	Fortitude and influence

IX. Hermit

Auspicious	Circumspection, solitude, searching, prudence
Inauspicious	Introvert, withdrawal, loneliness

> *If you're lonely when you're alone, youre in bad company.*
> —Jean-Paul Sartre

It is said that the human existence cannot receive spiritual inspiration except by quieting the humanity, the subconscious self, and the conscious self—only the superconscious self can attain wisdom. The Hermit attains wisdom by quieting these selves. In a positive placement, it represents time taken alone to seek advice from within or just to step back from hectic daily life. In a negative placement, the Hermit becomes introverted and removed; look to the card on the left to describe what is contributing to this.

Direction	Directional cue—left. The card to the left of the Hermit is what needs to be reflected upon (or what needs prudence). The card to the right of the Hermit explains what led to this.
Amplifies	Self-awareness and contemplation

X. Wheel of Fortune

Auspicious	Karma, fortune, luck, fluctuation, change
Inauspicious	Karma, bad luck, misfortunate events

The Wheel of Fortune spins in a continuous cycle, creating the ribbons of karmic actions that weave through human existence. Whether fortune falls in our favor or against us is determined by its placement within the spread. In a positive position, the Wheel of Fortune promises incredible changes that are fortunate in nature. When in a negative placement, we can expect karma to be repaid, but not in a good way, with past actions revisiting as karmic payback.

Direction	Stationary
Amplifies	Change and fated events

XI. Justice

Auspicious   Justice, equality, fair decisions

Inauspicious   Unfairness, decisions falling against us

Justice seeks the truth in a situation, remaining fair and unbiased at all times. When a situation is out of our own control, we hope that justice will be served. Justice speaks of legal or official matters, ones where a third party makes a decision that impacts our lives. When sitting ahead of the person's significator, Justice promises fairness and suggests that the situation will be decided in our favor. In a negative placement, Justice falls against us, and the situation feels gravely unjust.

Direction   Stationary

Amplifies   Fairness, for good or ill (the right thing will be done)

XII. The Hanged Man

Auspicious   Perspective, delay, trials, sacrifice

Inauspicious   Stasis, lengthy delays, unrealistic perspective

The man has been hanged by his ankle, suspended and left to watch the world go by from a standpoint that is both upside down and in stasis. Positively placed, the Hanged Man offers time and a new perspective to understand a situation. Negatively placed, the stasis of the Hanged Man is imposed, leading to delays and an unrealistic perspective of the situation as a whole.

Direction   Highlight. The Hanged Man highlights the card beneath; this card should be viewed with a newly gained perspective.

Amplifies   Perspective and sacrifice

XIII. Death

Auspicious   Death or end

Inauspicious   Death or end

The Death card foretells an ending and a failure of a situation that requires a period of grieving due to its severity. It is a card that can destroy hope and bring feelings of grief for the querent. When placed ahead of the person's significator, Death promises an ending that the querent will take in their stride despite its pain. When placed behind the person's significator, Death is an ending that is debilitating, exhausting, and worrisome. It is essential to look at the cards following the Death card to understand if the situation will transform into a new and more positive chapter for the querent. Remember, endings are very rarely comfortable, even when they lead to real positive change.

Direction	Movement. Death rides in from left to right, marking the ending of the situation in the card to the left. The card to the right of Death will explain what happens after the ending and where the querent is heading afterward. Only with positive cards following does Death show a positive end.
Amplifies	Endings and release

XIV. Temperance

Auspicious	Balance, moderation, maintenance, status quo
Inauspicious	Imbalance, excess, instability

It is time to stabilize the situation, practice moderation. and keep your approach balanced. A little bit of a good thing in moderation is welcomed, and Temperance speaks of situations in which we have to create the perfect blend of approaches in order to move forward. In a positive position, Temperance indicates that a balanced status quo is achieved in a situation. In a negative position, the situation is out of sync, and the two cards on either side are not in harmony with each other.

Direction	Highlight. Temperance mixes the cards left and right into the cups. See the flanking cards to understand what is being balanced.
Amplifies	Balance and moderation

XV. Devil

Auspicious	Temptation, manipulation, lust, addiction
Inauspicious	Urge, irresistible compulsion, oppression, force majeure

The master manipulator enters, leaving us in a quandary: Do we submit to temptation or use it to our own advantage? The Devil appears when we do not actively quell our fears or urges within a situation. It can speak of addictions or any of the seven deadly sins, pulling the flanking cards into a precarious situation. When positioned ahead of the person's significator, the Devil can be used to our advantage, manipulating a situation for our own benefit, or can just show that temptations will be overcome. Positioned behind the person's significator, the Devil reveals the worst of his attributes, signifying constraint and compulsions.

Direction	Highlight. The two people (echoing the Lovers card) draw the cards on the left and right into the situation of the Devil. These cards will explain the temptation or manipulation associated with the Devil.
Amplifies	Temptation and excess

XVI. The Tower

Auspicious	Chaos, adversity, calamity, catastrophe
Inauspicious	Ruin, destruction, devastation

A stormy outlook is foretold with the Tower card—the moment the world changes in the blink of an eye. Chaotic energy enters, and the constructs around us crumble to the ground. This can signify any moment of chaos in life, from accidents to relationship breakdowns; the Tower promises sudden turmoil of epic proportions. When placed ahead of the person's significator and surrounded by positive cards, the Tower represents ultimate positive disruption. Sometimes, we need to dismantle the constructs we have built to blast ourselves into the future, and the Tower highlights these situations. When placed behind the significator, it highlights chaos forced upon us from external sources, creating destruction in the querent's life.

Direction	Multihighlighted card. From the lightning strikes to the people falling, all the surrounding cards are hit with the chaos of the Tower and will explain the situation in full.
Amplifies	Chaos and ruin

XVII. The Star

Auspicious	Hope, prospects, guidance
Inauspicious	Despair, lack of prospects, pessimism

The light of hope in the night sky, the Star card offers a direction for those in need. Look to the cards surrounding the Star to navigate the situation. In a positive position, the Star is an optimistic sign that the querent will find a way forward. In a negative position, the Star leaves us void of direction and low on hope.

Direction	Stationary
Amplifies	Hope and direction

XVIII. The Moon

Auspicious	Deception, insecurities, hidden enemies
Inauspicious	Fraud, trickery, falsehoods, psychological/emotional manipulation

Moonlight hits the tableau and casts a shadow on the cards around, lulling them into a situation that is not all that it seems! Be wary when the Moon appears, for deception is foretold. When placed ahead of the person's significator, the Moon spotlights a situation that requires more research from the querent; dig deep and uncover the hidden information. When placed behind the person's significator, we must watch out for the darkest period of moonlight, casting the surrounding cards into a fraudulent or emotionally damaging situation.

Direction	Stationary
Amplifies	The unknown and deception

XIX. The Sun

Auspicious	Energetic, positive, sunny outlook
Inauspicious	Toxic positivity, overly optimistic, heat

The Sun brings energy into the tableau and promises that our endeavors will be successful. Promising betterment and happy days to come. In a positive position, the Sun shines on all the cards around, offering encouragement and favor. In a negative position, the Sun's warmth begins to scorch, and we are warned of being overly optimistic in a situation.

Direction	Stationary
Amplifies	Energy and positivity

XX. Judgment

Auspicious   Judgment, assessment, evaluation

Inauspicious   Bad judgment, a negative outcome

The final judgment is seen, and our rights and wrongs are laid on the table—a call from the universe where we await the verdict. The Judgment card shows a situation culminating in a final judgment of our worthiness. In a positive position, we can be sure that it will fall in our favor; however, in a negative placement, the final judgment is difficult to swallow. It is a card of consequences based on our actions or inactions. It could also show that you are awakening to the truths of the universe, assessing and evaluating at a cosmic level.

Direction   Stationary

Amplifies   Evaluation and judgments

XXI. The World

Auspicious   Completion, success, cycle ends

Inauspicious   Lack of achievement, disappointing end

Achievement, fulfillment, and completion at last—the World card brings a sense of conclusion to all the surrounding cards. The World appears in a positive placement when we are tangibly seeing the results of our manifestations and accomplishments. In a negative placement, the completion is not all it seems, and feels lackluster when it arrives.

Direction   Stationary

Amplifies   Completion and success

The Minor Arcana

The Minor Arcana features our daily lives and experiences. It represents the mundane, run-of-the-mill occurrences, from going to work to meeting with friends. The four suits (Cups, Swords, Wands, and Pentacles) highlight life areas in which daily occurrences happen.

The Suits

The suit of WANDS (FIRE)
Creativity, primal energy, spirituality, inspiration (superconscious self)

The suit of CUPS (WATER)
Emotions, relationships, feelings, connections (subconscious self)

The suit of SWORDS (AIR)
Intellect, brain power, attitudes (conscious self)

The suit of PENTACLES (EARTH)
Physical, material, realization, prosperity (human self)

The Courts

The Court cards (King, Queen, Knight, and Page) perform the most-important roles within a tableau spread. They highlight the dynamics of interpersonal relationships and indicate whether the future is favorable for the querent. A King or Queen chosen as a significator becomes the starting point for the querent's life story, focusing our attention when we read. The beauty of Tarot within a tableau is that it offers us the opportunity to delve into convoluted situations, involving multiple people, whilst simultaneously identifying their motivations and intentions. Each Court card has a personality and a "core essence" meaning. The core essence keywords explain what the Court card represents when it is not depicting a physical person. In small spreads, Court cards often indicate the qualities of those cards. However, in a tableau reading, where multiple layers of cards are laid, the Court cards almost always represent people. Take note of whether Knights and Pages land behind the King's or Queen's back, for the momentum and communication they refer to will become arduous for the querent.

- The Kings and Queens will dictate the narrative by using their directional cues and signify the querent and their partner.

- The Knights dictate actions within their directional cues.

- The Pages foretell of messages to be relayed or received.

The meanings below include the core essence and personality type of each card, along with keywords for an inauspicious placement in relation to the King or Queen significator (if that Court card is not your significator).

THE PAGES

In a tableau spread, the Pages are the youngest member of the court cards, bringing energy and chatter. If you are reading for a family, the Pages will spotlight anyone under twenty-five years old (male or female). However, their true tableau magic lies in their communication styles, serving as messengers of their suit. The directional quality of the Page (left or right facing) will determine the source of the message (perhaps who sent it or the subject thereof) and how the information will affect the querent's life. It is also important to note that the suit of the attending Page will confirm the type of message. For example, the Page of Cups will bring romantic messages, while the Page of Pentacles will deliver work or financial messages.

The card behind the Page is the source of the message; the card ahead of the Page is the outcome that message will have for the querent.

Message Source

Outcome

Outcome

Message Source

Page of Wands

THE INSPIRED MESSENGER

Auspicious   Inspired, artistic, excited
Inauspicious   Distracted, hasty, impatient, unreliable
Direction   Right facing

The youngest creative of the Wands Court, they are filled with inspiration and eager to get started. This can be any young man or woman who is creative, constantly trying new hobbies with an artistic flair. It is also worth noting that this Page often appears when we are excited about a new project and racing to get going! As a person, they are fun, energetic, and creative. In interpersonal relationships, this Page can represent anyone who is not yet classified as a Knight; they can be gregarious, full of banter, and ready for an adventure. The card behind the Page of Wands (to the left) is the incoming message or subject thereof, while the card to the right shows the outcome of that message. If the Page of Wands sits behind the King or Queen significator, the message being conveyed could be unreliable!

Page of Cups

THE ROMANTIC MESSENGER

Auspicious   Idyllic, dreamer, crush
Inauspicious   Immature, naive, insecure
Direction   Left facing

The youngest Cup person, the Page is full of youthful emotions. A sensitive individual, open, loving, and taking pleasure in the arts—think of a teenager full of the joys of their emotional well-being. The Page of Cups is a bit less worldly than their peers, enjoys a rose-tinted view of society, and seems to be in a world of their own. When the Page of Cups attends, think about the situation from a simpler viewpoint and ask yourself, How does it make you feel? As a messenger, the card behind the Page of Cups (to the right) shows the subject of the information arriving, while the card ahead (to the left) explains how this information will affect the querent's life. In a negative aspect to the significator card, the Page of Cups becomes immature and ignorant.

Page of Swords

THE INTELLECTUAL MESSENGER

Auspicious   Witty, thinker, information junkie, communicative
Inauspicious   Stalker, gossipy, sarcastic
Direction   Left facing

Imagine a superintelligent and chatty teen, both clever and curious, always bringing the latest gossip to your door. The Page of Swords is dynamic and engaging; they know how to flirt and use language to their advantage. They are adept at coming up with ideas for themself and their friends and loves a good debate. At their best, they are witty and a delight at any party; at their worst (in an inauspicious position), they become snarky and sarcastic and have an extremely sharp tongue. The message that the Page of Swords brings to the table is one of ideas of actions to be taken; just do not trust these too much when landing inauspiciously!

Page of Pentacles

THE INDUSTRIOUS MESSENGER

Auspicious   Diligent, ambitious, consistent, student, colleague
Inauspicious   Irresponsible, missed chances, lazy
Direction   Right facing

The youngest of the Pentacle people, the Page of Pentacles embodies the qualities of the suit; they are practical and studying their craft. With diligence to the task at hand and pure focus on the required outcome, the Page has a more mature outlook than their peers, demonstrating determination beyond their years. As the messenger of labor, the Page of Pentacles can bring news of job offers and financial advancement. However, beware when the Page of Pentacles lands in an inauspicious position, since it speaks of recklessness, irresponsibly, and missed opportunities.

THE KNIGHTS

The Knights are active and dynamic; they enter the spread with gusto and bring momentum to any situation shown. As people, the Knights embody the core essence of their suits and represent a person between the ages of twenty-five and fortyish. The most effective tableau technique is to employ the Knights as "action" and "movement" cards; that is to say, a Knight attending would confirm what movement can be expected. Each Knight will bring forth action within the core essence of their suit. For example, the Knight of Cups will enter with emotional movement, the Knight of Swords will enter with conscious action, the Knight of Wands will land in a spread when creative movement is foreseen, and the Knight of Pentacles will attend with practical momentum.

Start	Development

Development	Start

The card behind the Knight explains how the movement begins (or which situation is dynamic in the time frame), and the card ahead of the Knight confirms how the situation will develop. If four Knights attend, the situation is highly changeable and extremely active.

You can also consider the directional qualities of the Knights and their relation to the significator card. If the Knight is facing eye to eye with the King or Queen significator, it is an action that is incoming (an external force entering the querent's life). Should the Knight face in the same direction as the significator and in an auspicious position, this indicates direct actions of the querent.

Knight of Wands

THE MOMENTUM OF PASSION

Auspicious	Enthusiasm, drive, journeys
Inauspicious	Volatile, arrogant, reckless
Direction	Left facing

The active Knight of Wands oozes enthusiasm and drive, catapulted forward by his passions. He is a campaigner, motivated for a cause, and justly driven.

The Knight of Wands brings in fast-paced creative action and is always full of life. He can show that movement is heading the way of the client, with journeys and travel possible. The card landing behind the Knight of Wands (to the right) shows the start of the action or what movement is entering the querent's life, and the card to the left shows the outcome of the movement. Beware of the Knight of Wands sitting behind the significator's back, for he becomes volatile and domineering.

Knight of Cups

THE MOMENTUM OF LOVE

Auspicious   Charming, lover, romantic
Inauspicious   Vain, overemotional, moody
Direction   Right facing

Knights are always on the go, striving to be the best in their suit. They are seekers, finding their way in life. As a seeker of the suit of Cups, the Knight of Cups is someone seeking romance or a sign that a lover is on the way. He is loving and kind in his movement, completely in tune with his emotions and intuition. The card behind (to the left) shows what emotional action is entering, the card ahead (to the right) explains the outcome of this action. When positioned behind the significator, the Knight of Cups becomes vain and overemotional, spoiling the moment with tantrums or outbursts.

Knight of Swords

THE MOMENTUM OF DEBATE

Auspicious   Assertive, ambitious, mediator, speaker
Inauspicious   Rude, vicious, ruthless
Direction   Left facing

The Knight of Swords enters in dynamic flow, rushing in to solve any problems you may (or may not) have. Incredibly quick-witted and opinionated, he has a comeback for anything you throw at him, and commands a room upon entering. Action will always attend with the Knight of Swords; look to the card behind his back to understand what dynamic situation is entering and how that will affect the querent's life (the card ahead). In an inauspicious position, beware of the Knight of Swords, since his tongue becomes vicious and the arriving action could lead to arguments!

Knight of Pentacles

THE MOMENTUM OF FINANCIAL GROWTH

Auspicious	Practical, reliable, hardworking employee
Inauspicious	Cheap, workaholic, delay
Direction	Right facing

The Knight of Pentacles moves more slowly than his peers, but he enters with purpose, and you can trust in his ability to focus on the required duties. He works relentlessly and with diligence, always performing to the best of his abilities. Extremely practical, the Knight of Pentacles promises momentum in our endeavors, albeit a slow but sure approach. In an inauspicious position, however, the Knight of Pentacles focuses too hard on tasks until they consume him. A workaholic streak flows through his veins, making him blinkered in his duties. Moreover, the presence of the Knight of Pentacles inauspiciously is a sure sign that the situation will be delayed or, at the very least, progress at a painstakingly slow pace—an uphill battle!

QUEEN of WANDS. QUEEN of CUPS. QUEEN of SWORDS. QUEEN of PENTACLES.

THE QUEENS

The Queens are the representatives in the Tarot deck, attending with personalities befitting their core essence meaning and highlighting the very best qualities of their suit. Each Queen can be used as a significator for your client (when female) or the partner. **A Queen will rarely attend the tableau solely for their core essence meaning; they will almost always represent people within the querent's life.**

Queen of Wands

THE REPRESENTATIVE OF INDEPENDENT CREATIVITY

Auspicious	Confident, creative, passionate
Inauspicious	Challenging, vengeful, oppressive
Direction	Right facing
Partner	King of Wands or Queen of Cups / Queen of Pentacles (for same-sex readings)

Female significator who is confident, driven by inspiration, independent, and creative. A well-respected creative lady, a passionate and optimistic leader. The Queen of Wands represents her suit with extreme focus and passion; she will motivate and stand up for you at every opportunity. She may seem to be a little self-centered at times, but if you need someone to fire you up, the Queen of Wands is the person of choice. If the Queen of Wands lands in a negative aspect to the significator, the relationship between the two people is challenging, with the Queen of Wands becoming harsh and domineering.

Queen of Cups

THE REPRESENTATIVE OF COMFORT

Auspicious	Ally, counselor, friend
Inauspicious	Needy, overly sensitive, clingy
Direction	Left facing
Partner	King of Cups or Queen of Wands / Queen of Swords (for same-sex readings)

The Queen of Cups embodies the fluidity of her water associations and is empathic, caring, and very much in tune with her subconscious self. As a representative of emotions and intuition, the Queen of Cups has depth and fluidity of being. She can quell emotional turmoil with sound advice and can aid the querent to have faith in their intuition. The cards ahead of the Queen of Cups (to the left) will explain the focus of the querent in the set time frame, while the cards behind (to the right) will be more troublesome. Should the Queen of Cups land in an inauspicious placement, she becomes extremely needy, overly emotional, and somewhat fickle.

Queen of Swords

THE REPRESENTATIVE OF OPINIONS

Auspicious   Objective, professional, honest, sharp
Inauspicious   Malicious, bitter, bitchy
Direction   Right facing
Partner   King of Swords or Queen of Cups / Queen of Pentacles (for same-sex readings)

Eloquent and very sure of the power of her words, the Queen of Swords is knowledgeable and, some might say, opinionated. She commands the attention of those around and rules her subordinates with professional dynamism. Always honest and straight to the point, the Queen of Swords does not mince her words—what she says, she means. There will be no apologies for tones of voice or unsolicited advice. When landing in an inauspicious position, the Queen of Swords turns sour and greets the querent with malicious words or a hard-faced, ice-cold position.

Queen of Pentacles

THE REPRESENTATIVE OF OPERATIONS

Auspicious   Industrious, self-sufficient, generous
Inauspicious   Materialistic, intolerant, greedy
Direction   Left facing
Partner   King of Pentacles or Queen of Wands / Queen of Swords (for same-sex readings)

The Queen of Pentacles is very much connected with the earthly sign of the suit and her surroundings. She is a practical and helpful queen who takes responsibility for her role and leverages it for the common good. Financially secure and family-centric, the Queen of Pentacles nurtures those around her with duty and care. We can be sure that the Queen of Pentacles strives for financial stability for her citizens and will be unwavering in her loyalty and support. In an inauspicious position, the Queen of Pentacles loses her nurturing side and focuses on the money, becoming materialistic and greedy in her actions.

KING of WANDS.   KING of CUPS.   KING of SWORDS.   KING of PENTACLES.

THE KINGS

The Kings are the rulers in the Tarot deck. They lead by example and embody the core essence of their suits to succeed. Kings can be used as the significator card for your querent (when male) or as the partner card. **Kings rarely attend a tableau solely as the pure essence of the card's meaning; they will almost always represent a person within the querent's life.**

King of Wands

THE RULER OF INSPIRATION

Auspicious	Motivating, inspiring, extrovert
Inauspicious	Forceful, tyrant, dictator
Direction	Left facing
Partner	Queen of Wands or King of Cups / King of Pentacles (for same-sex readings)

If you need a motivational speaker, the King of Wands fits the role perfectly. He inspires those around him as a natural leader. An extroverted leader, he inspires his subjects in an authoritative yet encouraging manner. In addition, he moves with determination, ensuring that every project will be completed to his high standards, and nothing less will be accepted. If the King of Wands sits behind the significator, he brings his worst traits to the table, forcing his concepts on others, dictating direction, and pressurizing the querent to follow his methods of completion.

King of Cups

Auspicious   Family man, advisor, supporter
Inauspicious   Cold, manipulative, emotionally controlling
Direction   Right facing
Partner   Queen of Cups or King of Wands / King of Swords (for
                    same-sex readings)

The King of Cups, like all kings, is the leader of his suit. His leadership is determined by his water associations and the sensitive nature of someone in touch with their subconscious self. He is loving, supportive, and very much in control of his emotions—able to harness them and use them for good. "Lead by example, not by force" is his motto. The cards ahead (to the right) of the King of Cups will be auspicious, the cards behind (to the left) will be inauspicious. When placed behind the significator, the King of Cups uses the emotions of those around him for his own betterment, becoming cold and manipulative in his efforts.

King of Swords

THE RULER OF FACTS

Auspicious   Integrity, strategist, analytic, serious
Inauspicious   Irrational, harsh, controlling, power hungry
Direction   Left facing (in order to face his partner, we utilize
                    a left-facing rule)
Partner   Queen of Swords or King of Cups / King of Pentacles
                    (for same-sex readings)

Intelligent and analytical, the King of Swords considers his role as somebody who is fair and always seeks factual evidence. He speaks with intent and expects to be heard. The King of Swords is a born leader who thrives under pressure and prioritizes strategy over intuition. If you need solid strategic advice, the King of Swords will oblige. In an inauspicious position, the King of Swords becomes harsh and controlling in his verbiage, relentless until he has beaten the competitors and come out victorious.

King of Pentacles

THE RULER OF PROVISION

Auspicious	Abundant, secure, ambitious, patriarchal, assiduous
Inauspicious	Possessive, exploitative, financial control
Direction	Right facing
Partner	Queen of Pentacles or King of Wands / King of Swords (for same-sex readings)

The King of Pentacles is earthly, stable, and a solid investor. His number one priority is material security and the abundance of the earth around him. His role as protector and provider is met with enthusiasm and ambition, a King we can trust to be responsible and generous. We would see the King of Pentacles as the figurehead and CEO of a large corporation, leading the company with a solid foundation of hard work and determination. When placed inauspiciously to the significator, the King of Pentacles becomes possessive and controlling. He does not work well with others and tends to use his influence to serve his own purposes.

The Pips

Cards numbered 1 to 10 in each suit are called the pips. They explain everyday situations and actions to take. These were often read in accordance with numerology and increasing presence of the suit's core meaning. In the Rider-Waite deck, we hold on to this value while exploring pictorial cues. Within the core meanings below, the directional cue of a card is discussed, along with the practicalities of its application in interpretation.

The meanings below also contain keywords that will help build your narrative, along with a description of any movement shown within the imagery to augment your interpretations within a tableau. Keeping the core meaning short and concise will be helpful for a tableau-style narrative. Each card meaning includes an interpretation based on the placement of the card in an auspicious (positively aspected ahead of the significator) position or an inauspicious (negatively aspected behind the significator's back) position.

The pips in the Tarot deck can be read in conjunction with the number of the suit, and in the tableau, it is referred to as the wheel of evolution, a self-contained path for the emergence of self within the ethereal (spirit) and physical (human body). It represents where we came from, who we are, and who we will become, with each number within the pips adding supplementary interpretations. The more of the same number that attends in a cluster, the more prevalent the "number energy" becomes. The wheel of evolution provides a comprehensible order by which we can find the path of love from the light, through the darkness, and back into the light.

The wheel of evolution begins with the number zero, the time at which we are in our ethereal state. No matter what your belief system is, the number zero refers to the state in which we are at one with the universe, pure spirit and with no human traits. We do not have a single card within the pips that equates to the pure zero, because the pips are referencing our daily human lives. The concept of zero appears in the Major Arcana, our spiritual pursuits.

We will now begin our path of evolution in conjunction with the pips. Our spiritual praxis is the tenet by which we are released from our spiritual essence (in spirit) onto the earth realms (as humans); each step along the praxis is a step toward enlightenment.

ONE

The number one represents the moment of birth into human existence. We are taken from pure ethereal love and light into the confines of a human body, taking our first breath of air and starting on a new journey with the gift of free will and individuality.

The Aces in the pips highlight this moment of birth into the world and the first spiritual praxis, which speaks of individual experience, finding identity whilst learning to be self-sufficient and self-aware. In this vein, the Aces spotlight newness, originality, and seeds of self-awareness that can be sown to manifest. Moreover, we are born pure, with no preconceived ideas of the world or life. The Aces embody that moment of purity within the essence of the suits: pure inspiration (Wands), pure emotion (Cups), pure thought (Swords), and physical perfection (Pentacles), untainted by any external experiences.

When all four aces land in a tableau, it is a year of new starts and brand-new opportunities on the horizon!

ACE OF WANDS

Auspicious   New inspiration / drive / spark of creativity

The Ace of Wands is a spark of inspiration at a time when we need a creative solution or seed to sow. Divine insight when we need it the most, the Ace of Wands is the moment that your focus and intention combine to manifest the best possible outcome for you. Suddenly, you are drawn to action, compelled to follow your dreams. The Ace of Wands enters suddenly, a lightbulb moment that stokes the flames of your imagination. Suddenly you are drawn to action, compelled to follow your dreams.

Inauspicious   Unfulfilled inspiration, recklessness

Inauspiciously placed, the Ace of Wands suggests that we are not listening to the voice in our head urging us to act. The spark is there, but nobody is driving it forward! If you have a love or hobby that you are not pursuing, the Ace of Wands will appear negatively placed. Beware, too, of rash actions taken on a whim when this card is placed negatively!

Movement   None

ACE OF CUPS

Auspicious   New emotions, spark of feelings, new relationship

The hand offers a cup overflowing with water, an offer of new emotions and fresh experiences that cause excitement. The first butterflies when you cast your eyes on the perfect partner—think about how the spark of a new relationship makes you feel . . . That! The Ace of Cups is a beautiful card representing the newness of feelings in any situation, capturing a childlike simplicity in the love it holds.

Inauspicious   Emotional, flaky, feeling unloved

In an inauspicious position, the Ace of Cups becomes overly emotional in a naive and childlike state. When close to a significator in an inauspicious placement, this card can indicate flakiness.

Movement   None

ACE OF SWORDS

Auspicious   New ideas, thoughts, clarity, intellectual standpoint

New thoughts and ideas can be expected with the Ace of Swords. A decisive ability and clarity of thought dispel all the confusion in life. These are thoughts that bring action in life (for good or bad) and highlight our conscious new beginnings. The Ace of Swords offers the truth, the whole truth, and nothing but the truth.

Inauspicious   Highlights the truth in the inauspicious

The truth of the Ace of Swords will be heard; it may not be what you wanted to hear, but you will gain clarity about the situation. The Ace of Swords promises that you will learn with certainty what is really happening. Look at all the surrounding cards to understand what troublesome truth the querent is going to learn.

Movement   None

ACE OF PENTACLES

Auspicious   An opportunity, financial offer, resources

The Ace of Pentacles attends to present an offer of a brand-new cycle about to occur. Whether this manifests as a new job offer, a financial opportunity, or simply a fresh start, it is a new dawn and a chance to start from scratch. The Ace of Pentacles often attends when we are planting a seed for manifestation in the physical realm, the theoretical becoming tangible and real.

Inauspicious   Missed opportunities, meager offers

When in an inauspicious placement, the Ace of Pentacles suggests that an opportunity has been missed, or the offer itself is not substantial enough to bring happiness. It could signify a job offer that requires compromise, or indicate that we simply are not paying attention when opportunities arise.

Movement   None

TWO

The number two stands for polarity and duality, highlighting that we are not alone in this incarnation and that we must learn by experience on this earthly journey. While the number one began the journey with our individuality, learning to accept ourselves and even finding excitement for the path ahead, the number two reminds us that we are not on this journey alone. The second spiritual praxis is the law of polarity; namely, "We gain experience only in the reflection of opposites." In the lesson of the number two, we see our fellow journeyers and embrace the difference and similarities between ourselves. In this way, we learn more about ourselves and the power of duality.

All the twos ask us to look at the reflection of opposites in order to progress: the Two of Wands speaks of the need to see the future in the present, the Two of Swords addresses the difficulties within self when presented with a different idea, the Two of Cups emphasizes the necessity of expressing and giving emotions to be open to receiving love, and the Two of Pentacles highlights the dual roles that we need to keep in balance.

TWO OF WANDS

Auspicious   Planning, first steps, future plans, laying the groundwork

The Two of Wands is the calm before the action, emphasizing careful and detailed planning before stepping out into the unknown. It is a time for forethought and setting goals rather than immediate action. Take a step back, view the situation, and think it through thoroughly before committing. Restock, reappraise, and then plan the steps required to achieve the fulfillment of your dreams.

Inauspicious   Overanalyzing, nonaction, limbo

In a negative position, the Two of Wands indicates inaction and perhaps too much focus on future plans without sufficient elbow grease applied. It appears when we are procrastinating about what we cannot do, rather than motivating ourselves to act.

Movement   None; whilst he is looking to the horizon, no movement is seen.

TWO OF CUPS

Auspicious   Two people coming together, partnership, attraction

After the initial excitement at finding your "one," the relationship is solidified in mutual admiration. The Two of Cups promises beautiful connections, attraction, and union, bringing two souls together. In a work-themed reading, the Two of Cups suggests successful collaborations or agreements with others. Do not be surprised that the Two of Cups doesn't always speak of loving relationships!

Inauspicious   Separation, imbalance, division, unhealthful connections

In an inauspicious placement, the Two of Cups becomes worrisome, speaking of separations as well as unhealthful relationships and connections with others. An imbalance of emotions is presented that will destabilize the relationship. If the card is surrounded by positive cards (despite its inauspicious position), it suggests inappropriate flirting or a situation that initially appears innocent but, on second glance, is not so!

Movement   None

TWO OF SWORDS

Auspicious   Difficult decisions, choices, stalemate, indecisiveness

The Two of Swords attends with two opposing ideas. The blindfolded figure does not know which option is the best, and sits in limbo while that decision is made. She sits alone, her senses heightened by the blindfold, and must rely on her intellect to choose the right option. When we fail to make decisions, we become passive in our own lives. This inactivity can lead to feelings of being overwhelmed. The Two of Swords pleads with the querent to be decisive and take an active role in their own narrative!

Inauspicious   Confusion, ambiguity, dithering

There is no winner when the Two of Swords lands inauspiciously to your significator. The levels of indecisiveness rise and confusion reigns, turning your querent into a dithering mess. Decisions become anxiety-producing and a real sticking point in the situation.

Movement   None

TWO OF PENTACLES

Auspicious   Multitasking, keeping the equilibrium, multiple responsibilities

The Two of Pentacles depicts a person juggling two coins, signifying the moments when we need to juggle our responsibilities to remain in control. Whether your to-do list requires fine balancing skills to reach completion, or you just have a lot of chores on your radar that need to be synchronized, the Two of Pentacles helps you create equilibrium and flow through your workload with flair. The two cards flanking the Two of Pentacles will confirm what situation requires a careful balancing act.

Inauspicious   Unorganized, messy, imbalance

In an inauspicious position, the Two of Pentacles suggests that we are struggling to find balance in our daily lives. Workloads become unmanageable (especially with Nine of Wands nearby), and we fail to go with the flow. Keeping all our responsibilities in check becomes troublesome.

Movement   None

THREE

The journey of individuality and duality does not remove our remembrance of our ethereal selves, the separation from source. It is within the number three that the third spiritual praxis enters. It promises that through "wisdom, will, and love as an expression in the material," we will experience the permanent trinity, living as an individual yet incorporating duality and spirituality as one. In the threes, we incorporate the lessons learned with our peers and feel connected, not only on a human level but also with the spiritual self.

When all threes land within a tableau, we can be sure that we are operating within the physical realms but seeking expansion and experience to connect us spiritually. The Three of Wands speaks of expanding our horizons, the Three of Cups represents the merriment we experience with the trinity, the Three of Swords contains the pain of separation, and the Three of Pentacles emphasizes the necessity for all three aspects to be working in unison.

THREE OF WANDS

Auspicious   Progress, expansion / overseas opportunities / keep looking forward

The Three of Wands is the card of expansion and evolution. Standing on the shore, the figure looks out into the horizon, seeking world domination through the carefully laid plans in the Two of Wands. Progress and advancement are promised, along with advice to keep focusing on growth and development.

Inauspicious   Obstacles, delays, lack of growth

Inauspiciously placed, the Three of Wands throws obstacles in the path of expansion and slows down the growth you want to see! Understand that the situation may take some time to get off the ground.

Movement   None

THREE OF CUPS

Auspicious   Celebration, friendship, merriment

The Three of Cups depicts a celebration where chalices are raised. It is a happy card showing our well-being within our close circle of friends. The third person on the card brings in a sociable feeling and a time to have some fun! "Celebrate with your tribe" is the core essence of the Three of Cups, promising a pleasurable experience.

Inauspicious   Gossip, threesome, excess

Beware of the Three of Cups in an inauspicious position. It can indicate an unwanted third party, excess, love triangles, and gossipy friends. Pay particular attention when the Page of Cups also appears in an inauspicious position.

Movement   None

THREE OF SWORDS

Auspicious   Grief, sadness, loss, head over heart

The Three of Swords is a painful card signifying grief, hurt, betrayal, and sadness. Every moment of heartache is embodied in this card; perhaps intellectual arguments have turned into a shouting match of wicked proportions, with words used intentionally to pierce the feelings of those around us. Physical pain can also be shown, along with heartache, promising suffering and torment. One aspect we can learn from the Three of Swords is to process our emotional pain in the conscious mind and think logically rather than emotionally. In an auspicious position, the pain may be short lived.

Inauspicious   Pain, trauma, devastation

In an inauspicious position, the grief of the Three of Swords stings deeply. It signifies a painful and sometimes mortifying situation that we cannot avoid. It is personal, and we struggle to overcome the feeling that we have been betrayed.

Movement   None

Auspicious   Teamwork, sharing of the accomplishment, group responsibility

Three people on the card confer about the job at hand, assisting one another as three pentacles are placed, allowing them to finally enjoy the fruits of their labor. Do not confuse the Three of Pentacles with the Three of Cups, however; whilst the team celebrates their efforts, they highlight the importance of collaboration and working together. The Three of Pentacles promises fortunate collaborations and a strong team to help you reach your goals.

Inauspicious   Lack of teamwork, ineffective team, competition

In an inauspicious position, the Three of Pentacles suggests that our collaborations are not as effective as we believe. A lack of cohesion between team members needs to be addressed. It can also indicate that the team is working against one another. The Three of Pentacles can likewise attend when the querent finds there are one too many fingers in the pie; too many cooks spoil the broth!

Movement   None

FOUR

The fourth spiritual praxis is referred to as the "four faces of god" or tetractys (which symbolizes the four classical elements of air, fire, water, and earth), also known as the formula for eternal life. Fours stand for Earth, the physical body, and the four classical elements: air, fire, water, and earth. A perfect balance of earthly components, we have incorporated individuality, duality, and trinity into our lives, feeling the benefits of the manifestations we have sown in the material world.

The fours promise that we have found a sense of stability within and outside ourselves and are enjoying our earthly lives. Even the Four of Cups, which leans on the negative scale of cards, confirms that we have a foundation—but perhaps one that we are not yet completely happy with!

FOUR OF WANDS

Auspicious   Stability, easy, social gatherings

The Four of Wands promises a period of stability, a time when we can enjoy the creative flow and appreciate our passions. Whether you are enjoying moments with like-minded people or hanging out with your friends and family, the Four of Wands promises a pleasurable occasion.

Inauspicious   Contentious gatherings, instability

If the 4 of Wands falls in an inauspicious placement, it becomes unstable and rocks our foundation—especially with others. Beware of discord among family and friends and a time of instability.

Movement   None

FOUR OF CUPS

Auspicious   Apathy, boredom, "not enough," contemplation

Taking a step back from the limelight, the Four of Cups is not entirely interested in any offers coming forth. He sits, bored of his lot, pondering why life is so mundane. A card of inaction and retreat, the Four of Cups highlights times when we just cannot be bothered! In an auspicious placement, we can expect to feel unexcited and uninspired in our daily lives, as if we are living the same monotonous day over and over again, like a Groundhog Day with no relief in sight.

Inauspicious   Indifference, melancholy, depression

In an inauspicious position, the Four of Cups becomes sullen and retreats from any invitations, sinking into a cloud of melancholy. With other cards to substantiate, the querent could be suffering emotionally.

Movement   None

FOUR OF SWORDS

Auspicious   Rest, mental timeout, meditation, hold that thought!

It is time to set your swords down and give yourself a well-deserved mental break. The swords are parked, no battles are being fought right now, and it is time to sit back and relax. We are most susceptible to attack when sleeping, but we must allow ourselves to feel vulnerable in order to replenish our reserves. The Four of Swords can be a warning that a mental break is required or just a confirmation that the mental onslaught isn't serving you well.

Inauspicious   Burnout, exhaustion, collapse

In an inauspicious position, the Four of Swords becomes an enforced timeout, a situation that creates a need to retreat and take stock. It can also signify that we are too laid back, which is having a negative effect on our well-being. Beware when the Death card falls close to the Four of Swords, since it could indicate the possibility of an actual fatality.

Movement   None

FOUR OF PENTACLES

Auspicious   Protecting investments, holding on to your assets, hoarding

There are times in life that we feel the need to slow down and hold on to everything we have attained, both material and emotional, fearing that moving forward would rock the boat and deplete some of our precious resources. Whilst it is admirable to save and invest, the Four of Pentacles speaks of a tight rein on our lives, protecting our investments, stability, and security. In an auspicious position, the Four of Pentacles highlights a time when we need to focus on what we have attained and protect it going forward.

Inauspicious   Possessiveness, hoarding, a firm grip

In an inauspicious position, the Four of Pentacles confirms that we have a firm grip on our situation, but suggests that we are too rigid in our position. Holding on so tightly that our knuckles turn white, this can apply to anything in life—from relationships to career paths—illustrating the struggle to cling to our position.

Movement   None

FIVE

The number five stands for free will and individuality. Unlike the number one, where we experience our individuality as a single entity, the fives show that we are experiencing our individuality within the company of duality, polarity, and opposites. The fifth spiritual praxis is one of vibration, frequency, and momentum—we have the ability to apply free will, but we have to apply it in an existence where every individual has the right to do the same. This can cause confusion and discord within our lives.

The fives bring external influence on our free will and challenge how we react when our individual belief system is rocked: the Five of Wands highlights discord, the Five of Cups disappointment, the Five of Swords conflict, and the Five of Pentacles adversity.

FIVE OF WANDS

Auspicious   Competition, disagreements, discord, tension

Differing viewpoints often cause conflicts between creative and passionate people, and how we deal with our reactions in adverse situations of discord can be reflected in the Five of Wands. Never a positive card, the Five of Wands always brings friction and resistance within a situation. However, with positive cards around, it could indicate a healthful brainstorming exercise!

Inauspicious   Rivalry, nasty arguments, battlelines

In an inauspicious placement, the Five of Wands can turn downright nasty, creating disharmony among the surrounding cards. Aggressive behavior, physical altercations, and heated debates are all examples of this.

Direction   None

FIVE OF CUPS

Auspicious   Disappointment, regrets, loss, a sinking feeling

The figure in the Five of Cups cannot contain his disappointment and dissatisfaction at the spoils beneath his feet. His physical body is drooped, head lowered, shoulders hung, full of regret and consumed with what went wrong. He stands still, clinging to the past, afraid to walk forward into the future. The Five of Cups attends at times of disappointment or personal failure, highlighting that the past is overinfluencing the present.

Inauspicious   Grief, anguish, sorrow

Disappointment lowers our emotional well-being, and when placed in an inauspicious position, the loss turns to grief and sorrow of overwhelming proportions. This is a painful card in which the querent sits and wallows, afraid to let go when it is time to move on.

Movement   None

FIVE OF SWORDS

Auspicious   Conflict, arguments, winning in dubious circumstances, stress

There are no winners or losers with the Five of Swords, for both sides have suffered losses and each is conflicted. This card often signifies intellectual premises and beliefs that have become the cause of arguments, leading to hostility and lines being drawn. The Five of Swords suggests that while you may feel you have come out on top, the victory is bittersweet.

Inauspicious   Hostility, intimidation, aggression

In an inauspicious position, the Five of Swords becomes more hostile, indicating situations wherein conflict turns nasty. The fight may feel unfair, and sides become blurred. It is time to walk away and lick your wounds.

Movement   None

FIVE OF PENTACLES

Auspicious   Lack, adversity, struggle, hardship

The Five of Pentacles casts a bleak outlook in a spread, promising that we will experience adversity and it won't be pleasant. There is an overriding sense that we just don't have enough (money, health, land, etc.). When the Five of Pentacles lands in an auspicious placement, we can expect hardships to arrive. Look to the card to the left to understand which life area this affects.

Inauspicious   Insolvency, unemployment, loss

In an inauspicious position, the Five of Pentacles is quite bleak. It represents a situation wherein we experience despair at our position, possibly facing unemployment, insolvency, or a loss of status. This difficult card in a difficult position amplifies the situation to a miserable existence; it is essential to examine the card on the left to find the source of this suffering.

Movement   Moving left to right, the adversity begins with the card to the left, and the outcome will be shown in the card to the right.

SIX

The sixth spiritual praxis confirms that we are moving away from the external confrontation of our individuality in the five and gaining a deeper understanding of the darkness within and outside ourselves. The number six speaks of the absence of light after conflict or difficult times, when we are troubled by our own actions and have found our own darkness within our behavior during these times; however, it is within that darkness that we can experience the light. We all must strive to understand the intricacies of our own darkness in order to succeed and thrive in life, and the sixes in Tarot teach us that out of our own experience of darkness, we can strive into the light. The external adversity of the fives has caused us to understand our own position in conflicts. It is here that we need to use this understanding of good, the bad, and the ugly to gain a grip and move forward.

The sixes speak of personal victory (Six of Wands), delving into the past (Six of Cups), moving on (Six of Swords), and sharing material wealth (Six of Pentacles), each card referencing our personal journey of self-acceptance in adversity. Every six has moved on from the distress of the five and transitioned from hardship into a better sense of being.

SIX OF WANDS

Auspicious   Victory, recognition, success

Riding into town, head held high, in a moment of victory, the Six of Wands foretells of success and a pride in our endeavors, whether in the work front or personal achievements. The Six of Wands promises that we will be able to hold our heads high in the face of adversity and trailblaze if necessary!

Inauspicious   Ill-gained success, meager recognition

In an inauspicious placement, the Six of Wands signifies that we are either celebrating victory too soon or that the success is not rightfully ours. At times, it may also be a sign that the recognition we seek is not being given to the extent we feel is deserved.

Movement   Rides to the right: the card on the right-hand side shows the outcome of the success.

SIX OF CUPS

Auspicious   Revisiting the past, memories, childhood, childlike

The Six of Cups is extremely sentimental, recalling fond moments in life and affectionately remembering lessons from our childhood. It also shows a child-like joy, urging us to stop taking life so seriously and to find contentment in the smaller joys of life. A playful card, when surrounded by positive cards the Six of Cups provides the freedom needed to grow and explore happy memories.

Inauspicious   Stuck in the past, childish, naive

In an inauspicious placement, this card indicates an unhealthful focus on the past, showing times when we may act childishly or in an ignorant manner.

Movement   None

SIX OF SWORDS

Auspicious   Transition, moving on, change, escape

The Six of Swords is a movement card, showing the querent moving away from a situation. However, it is a necessary move forward; the current situation is untenable—we must move beyond this and toward the future for our own sanity.

Inauspicious   Running away from problems, fleeing, absconding

In an inauspicious position, the Six of Swords acts more swiftly. It speaks of running away from the issues at hand and removing ourselves entirely from the life we have been living. In some cases, the Six of Swords can indicate that a hasty move has been made and that the direction is straying from the sensible.

Movement   The boat on the Six of Swords moves to the right. The card on the left-hand side shows what situation the querent is moving away from. The card on the right-hand side explains what situation the querent is moving toward.

SIX OF PENTACLES

Auspicious   Financial aid, sharing, giving, support

The Six of Pentacles speaks about the redistribution of wealth. Financial aid and recurring payments are highlighted with this card. In an auspicious placement, sharing is foreseen, and the querent can be sure their request for financial support will be granted. Similarly, donations, charity, and assistance could be given by the querent. The Six of Pentacles promises there is enough to go around and that everyone will receive their fair share.

Inauspicious   Oversharing, financial-aid rejection, less to go around

In an inauspicious position, the Six of Pentacles warns that we are overcompensating in our generosity. Oversharing and attention "bombing" can be suggested. In a financial reading, the Six of Pentacles inauspiciously will confirm that a loan will be rejected or that recurring payments are off the charts!

Movement   None

SEVEN

The seventh spiritual praxis speaks of the correspondences of the macro- and microcosmos, the free will of man in complete balance with spirit and the creator. Seven is both a magical and mystical number, frequently appearing in stories and the Bible, and is often associated with karmic lessons and manifestation. To harvest the rewards of our lessons learned, we must apply ourselves in the material world whilst closing karmic cycles. It can take a lifetime to work through many of our karmic lessons and recognize the trigger to finally respond in new ways rather than continuing old patterns. Every single person we interact with is following similar karmic patterns, and the sevens speak of our behaviors and our ability to see the problems that lie in front of us as we choose our reactions: the Seven of Wands reacts defensively yet gains the upper hand, the Seven of Cups responds with confusion yet sees the available opportunities, the Seven of Swords recognizes the deceit within the situation while calling it out, and the Seven of Pentacles focuses on personal growth and success over others.

SEVEN OF WANDS

Auspicious   Gain the upper hand, challenges, obstacles, defense

Sometimes life throws obstacles in our direction that we need to navigate or defend ourselves against, much like the arcade game "Whac-A-Mole," constantly batting back the next onslaught. The Seven of Wands often falls when we are striving to do our best; yet, whatever we do, something comes back to block our progress. Whether we are defending a position we have fought hard to achieve or trying to fend off the next chore, the Seven of Wands promises it will be a struggle.

Inauspicious   Insurmountable obstacles, interference, struggles

In an inauspicious position, the Seven of Wands becomes even more troublesome, and we feel we are fighting a losing battle. Obstacles arise, external influences interfere, and we are left depleted and battling every step of the way.

Movement   The Seven of Wands hits the card beneath with his wand. The card below highlights what the querent is trying to defend against.

SEVEN OF CUPS

Auspicious   Opportunities, options, daydreams, wishful thinking

It would be wonderful if we had the capacity to become emotionally involved in every opportunity that comes our way. Sadly, at times, we must choose between viable options rather than embrace everything. The Seven of Cups presents a multitude of directions and opportunities to capture your emotional interest. However, take time to consider the options. Don't be fooled by sparkly offerings; understand what they mean to you. Confusion abounds when options are bountiful; don't be distracted as you consider every aspect.

Inauspicious   Confusion, illusion, distractions

In an inauspicious position, the Seven of Cups creates distractions. Beware of confusion and overwhelming anxiety as you struggle to decide. Only you can decipher the true opportunities from the time wasters; do not fall for the smoke screen! It can also be a warning that you tend to become lost in your fantasies. Check the surrounding cards to confirm what distractions are present.

Movement   None

SEVEN OF SWORDS

Auspicious   Deception, lies, dishonesty, theft

The Seven of Swords is a dirty, deceitful card, highlighting times when we feel a stab of betrayal from our circle of trust. Sometimes we hide our intentions from others (for good or bad) and tell untruths to save our own behinds. The Seven of Swords will present when a person or situation is working against the best interest of our querent, spotlighting the betrayal as it occurs.

Inauspicious   Malicious, petty, spiteful, vengeance

Placed behind the significator, the Seven of Swords becomes more spiteful and personal in its betrayal. A person is acting maliciously, or a situation has moved from irritation to disgust. Decisions will be made against the querent that are unfair when the Justice card is nearby.

Movement   Left. The 7 of Swords steals from the card to the right and runs to the left.

SEVEN OF PENTACLES

Auspicious   Patience, "slowly, slowly, catchy monkey," sustainability, investment

The Seven of Pentacles highlights that the effort and investment we put into our lives will be rewarded with a little perseverance. It is a slow-acting card, promising that we will be rewarded if we can wait patiently for our seeds to manifest. In an auspicious position, the Seven of Pentacles guarantees that we will reap what we sow, and our hard work and persistence will not go unrecognized.

Inauspicious   Low yielding, setbacks, lack of growth

Inauspiciously placed, the Seven of Pentacles does not yield the harvest that we had hoped for. We may not have put in enough effort, or our impatience has caused setbacks and delays in our harvest.

Movement   None

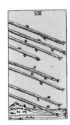   

EIGHT

The eighth spiritual praxis explains the relationship between cause and effect for the resurrection and mental overcoming of physical death. Through our understanding of karmic lessons in the sevens, we now allow our spirit to vibrate at a higher frequency, seeing both the cause of a situation and its effect. This understanding enables us to transform the world we live in through small actions of our own. The eights speak of infinity as all our lessons are learned, and we are ready to experience the fluidity of life. A situation can be very stale if unchanging, but with all eights attending, we can be sure it will become dynamic, albeit with the hint of "Slow down" from the Eight of Swords. The Eight of Wands attends with high energy and momentum, the Eight of Cups attends with self-confidence and the ability to walk away, the Eight of Swords attends with inaction and stickiness, and the Eight of Pentacles attends with an assured slow pace and quality.

Every situation we experience within the eights stems from shedding past lessons and reemerging from the ashes of our previous existence.

EIGHT OF WANDS

Auspicious   Momentum, speed, progress, motion

Eight wands glide majestically through the air, gaining momentum. Their trajectory explains the action further. A sudden yet balanced burst of energy enters the reading and creates movement in the cards around, drawing them into a dynamic situation. Beware, however, for this fast pace will also affect negative cards that are touching. For example, the conflict of the Five of Wands quickly morphs into physical fights. Alone and surrounded by positive cards, the Eight of Wands promises action and a fast-paced environment.

Inauspicious   Hasty, rash, poorly prepared

In an inauspicious placement, the Eight of Wands becomes hasty with an unmeasured response to the situation, speaking of poor planning and action without premise.

Movement   Traveling from left to right, wands show where the action begins (the card to the left) and where the action takes the querent (the card to the right).

EIGHT OF CUPS

Auspicious   "See you later, alligator!" "In a while, crocodile!"

Sometimes in life, we need to walk away from difficult or disappointing situations. We know that the grass is not always greener, but the situation itself is no longer viable. We stand tall, walk out, and move forward into unknown territory. The Eight of Cups holds his head high and walks off into the distance, leaving everything behind and focusing on the future.

Inauspicious   Abandonment, desertion, running away

In an inauspicious placement, the Eight of Cups storms out of the building rather than ambling away. Sudden abandonment or choosing to run away from a situation is shown. In this position, we cannot suggest that the grass will be greener on the other side; the desertion will have consequences.

Movement   The figure moves to the right. The card to the left explains the difficult situation, while the card to the right indicates whether the grass is greener on the other side!

EIGHT OF SWORDS

Auspicious   Restricted, trapped by circumstance, victim mentality

The Eight of Swords speaks of being trapped by circumstances of our own making, feeling restricted despite having all the freedom in the world. Sometimes we feel helpless and bound by the ties we have created, sensing that we have no form of control in the situation. In an auspicious position, we are afforded the ability to transform a victim mentality into a more empowering frame of mind.

Inauspicious   Imprisonment, powerless, paralyzed

In an inauspicious position, the Eight of Swords becomes an enforced restraint, a time when we cannot move forward. An external situation affects your own, creating a prisonlike existence fraught with mental anguish.

Movement   None

EIGHT OF PENTACLES

Auspicious   Practice, expertise, skill, high quality

Repetition builds perfection, and an essential part of our career paths is to become an expert in our field and masterful in our application. The Eight of Pentacles spotlights a time when we need to focus on the job at hand and practice until we consider ourselves masters. Treat your career, hobbies, and interests with the respect they demand and become a pro in your field.

Inauspicious   Rushed, lack of skills, lack of attention

The Eight of Pentacles inauspiciously shows that we are not paying due attention to the quality of our workmanship. Perhaps our skill set is not yet at the level we require, or we are simply not paying enough attention to our end product. The Eight of Pentacles asks that we consider our skill set and how to apply ourselves in order to improve.

Movement   None

NINE

After moving through the release of old patterns, we move into the nines and their spiritual lesson: that harmony must prevail in all energy exchanges. In other words, giving and receiving must always be in equilibrium for a person to be whole. The lessons we have learned on polarity and duality are revisited with the fresh understanding that we are both the cause and effect in our own universe, and within that universe, we receive the energy we expend. The nines attend when we are receiving our "payback" for energies expended. Whilst the Nine of Pentacles and Nine of Cups promise beautiful rewards, the Nine of Swords and Nine of Wands indicate that we will be burdened in mind and body. The nines are balanced within the four suits—two positives, two negatives—canceling one another out into equilibrium. Note, however, that whilst the nines do speak of payback, they are not referring to the ultimate manifestation, which is reserved for the tens.

NINE OF WANDS

Auspicious   Persistence, resilience, near completion, keep going, fatigue

The Nine of Wands shows that we have matured on our journey and have accumulated much along the way. We have been working toward our dreams for a long time, but those goals have not yet been met. The Nine of Wands advises that we have invested so much for such a long period that it is not time to give up. We may not have reached fruition, but we have won some battles along the way. It is time to dig deep, grit your teeth, and harness the determination to keep going.

Inauspicious   Stubbornness, resistance, exhaustion

In an inauspicious position, the Nine of Wands becomes rigid and stubborn, unable to see the woods for the trees. The cards around it will explain how this resistance is affecting the querent's situation.

Movement   Stationary

NINE OF CUPS

Auspicious   Satisfaction, self-reliance, rewards, having one's ducks in a row

Confidence and self-assurance ooze from the Nine of Cups, suggesting a contentment in our achievements to date. It is often referred to as the "wish" card; it suggests that the querent has worked hard to be able to enjoy their pursuits. You can be sure that your wishes will be fulfilled and that you will be satisfied that your life is in order. It is time to enjoy the rewards from the effort you have applied so far.

Inauspicious   Self-satisfying, stubbornly independent, keeping up
appearances

In an inauspicious placement, the Nine of Cups becomes quite selfish, satisfying self over others. Beware when the Two of Cups is also inauspiciously placed, since together they confirm a separation of two lovers, with the independence of one party to blame.

Movement   None

NINE OF SWORDS

Auspicious   Negativity, anxiety, worries

The dark night of the soul presents in the Nine of Swords. Anxiety-ridden thoughts permeate our existence, making us unable to think clearly or present ourselves as cohesively as we would like. The Nine of Swords brings existential crisis and an overload of thought processes, leaving the querent exhausted and incapable of rational thought.

Inauspicious   Depression, deep despair, misery

In an inauspicious position, the Nine of Swords becomes a deep despair and possible depression with burnout. Thoughts become illogical, and misery seeps into the very core of our being.

Movement   None

NINE OF PENTACLES

Auspicious   Enjoyment of wealth, attainment, luxury, independence

The Nine of Pentacles indicates the happiness, joy, and freedom that financial independence affords. It represents the luxury of not having to worry about our status because we have already put in the hard work. Now is the time to enjoy our leisure! In an auspicious position, the Nine of Pentacles is confident, affluent, and extremely enjoyable. It can signify spending good-quality time alone or an opportunity to pamper ourselves.

Inauspicious   Separation, singledom, ego, selfish, overspending

In an inauspicious position, the Nine of Pentacles becomes egotistical and selfish, looking after number one above all else. The presence of relationship cards (e.g., Two of Cups) nearby can confirm a relationship breakdown with a move into singledom. If financial cards are present (e.g., Six of Pentacles), this signifies overspending, rash purchases, and living beyond our means.

Movement   None

TEN

The tens highlight the law of abundance within our lives, the love and light of spirituality, which is then reflected in ourselves. Ten signifies the 1 (individuality) finally reunited with the 0 (source/creator) with a full culmination of the cycle. The ten aspects of spirituality as a sequence for understanding self within the cosmos have reached their culmination, and some would say that the law of abundance has taken its hold and the final manifestation has arrived. However, how has that manifestation presented in our lives? Whilst the nines speak of payback for energy expended, the tens speak of the ultimate end goal—a happily ever after, and the Ten of Pentacles and Ten of Cups will confirm this to you. However, the promises from the Ten of Swords and Ten of Wands that the suffering is ending do not come without the understanding that there may be some cycles needing to be revisited in order to attain the happiness of the Ten of Cups or affluence of the Ten of Pentacles.

TEN OF WANDS

Auspicious   Burden, responsibility, pressure, unable to see the
forest for the trees

The Ten of Wands promises that the battles that have been fought were not in vain—you have weathered the storm and collected war wounds, but you are still hanging in there! However, you have also accumulated more responsibilities along the way, which are weighing heavily on your shoulders. In an auspicious position, the Ten of Wands confirms that we acutely feel the burden of our circumstances; we bear that weight with determination.

Inauspicious   Overwhelming responsibility, feeling stuck

In an inauspicious position, the burdens become overwhelming—it is time to seek help with your responsibilities. Delegation is not easy, but those burdens need to be reorganized into more-manageable and bite-sized pieces so that you are not shouldering the responsibility alone.

Movement   A slow-moving card to the right. The card to the left explains the reason for the burdens, the card to the right shows what situation the burden will affect.

TEN OF CUPS

Auspicious   Emotional fulfillment, happiness, harmony

A rainbow graces the Ten of Cups, providing the backdrop for our emotional fulfillment. The Ten of Cups is the "happily ever after" card within the Tarot deck, promising happiness, joy, and, most importantly, harmony. It represents everything that we ever wished for being rolled up and gifted to us—a harmonious community, a happy family, the perfect day!

Inauspicious   Family discord, disharmony, dissension

In an inauspicious position, the Ten of Cups is worrisome; it speaks of discord within the family unit or disharmony within self that affects the broader community. If the Four of Wands is also present, we could be seeing the breakdown of a relationship.

Movement   None

TEN OF SWORDS

Auspicious   Pain, painful endings, loss, failure

Wrongs have not been righted, and the Ten of Swords presents the ultimate failure with a side order of betrayal. The imagery suggests that the querent has been stabbed in the back—it hurts, stings, and feels tortuous, but at least it's over . . . right? The Ten of Swords is painful even in an auspicious position. We won't escape unscathed, but we will understand that this is the absolute worst and can only get better!

Inauspicious   Ruin, disaster, stabbed in the back

Inauspiciously placed, the Ten of Swords amplifies in magnitude, and the earthquake you experience is tsunami-producing! The stab in the back becomes life ruinous and excruciatingly painful.

Movement   None

TEN OF PENTACLES

Auspicious   Stability, wealth, long-term success

The Ten of Pentacles provides total material fulfillment, a sense of permanence, and the satisfaction we feel when our long-term vision becomes tangible. It is a promise that everything will work out as planned, and that the hard work and effort expended will be rewarded. It is also a card of affluence, and essential in a financial reading to confirm the maturing of investments. The future is bright—just keep working toward your own perfect life.

Inauspicious   Fleeting success, unreachable goals, long-term prospects destroyed

In an inauspicious position, the Ten of Pentacles still holds its core essence of material fulfillment, but the shine is lost, leaving the querent with short-lived successes or unrealistic expectations for the perfect life and its attainability. It can also reveal instability in the querent's foundations.

Movement   None

Tarot Tableau Basics

Tableau Techniques

Tableau techniques have been used for generations. They merge the very best of our cartomantic traditions in order to interpret predictive readings. The core essence of each card (as detailed in "The Meanings" section) is utilized, allowing for the fluid merging of the core essences of all surrounding cards whilst employing the directional cues within your deck. Tableaus are a multilayered reading method and should be viewed as such, allowing you to add storylines by integrating extra techniques. It is not essential to use all techniques in a single tableau; begin with the first step and move on to the next when you are confident in your interpretations. "The Basic Tableau" information below will allow you to understand how the cards interact with one another, and the "Tableau Advanced" section includes all the steps you need to complete a comprehensive tableau reading.

The Basic Tableau

HOW TO CHOOSE A TABLEAU

There are many tableau spreads available to the reader. Below is a selection of six "Grand Tableau" styles to explore (using as few as thirty-two cards and as many as seventy-eight). It is not important which tableau style you start with; what's important is having fun and not being overwhelmed by so many cards. Each of the tableau layouts listed below can be read with the techniques beginning on page 81.

THE STANDARD TABLEAU, 8 × 4

The Standard Tableau layout is for the thirty-two-card playing-card deck and consists of eight cards per row, with four rows in total. The Standard Tableau is perfect for any predictive reading. With no "line of fate," you can read a simple narrative and delve into interpersonal relationships.

THE GRAND TABLEAU, 8 × 4 + 4

The most popular tableau spread contains thirty-six cards and includes a "line of fate" of four cards at the bottom. The additional four cards are perfect for understanding what is not going to happen within the set time frame. This can be especially useful if, for example, a querent has a question about timing, such as "When will I meet my next partner?" or "Will I get a promotion in the coming six months?" If significator cards for that life area land in the line of fate, you know it won't be within the set time frame. The 8 × 4 + 4 is my personal "go to" tableau because of the possible interactions between line of fate and the main reading.

THE GERMAN TABLEAU, 9 × 4

The German Tableau is a straightforward layout with nine columns and four rows. It is the same format as the Standard Tableau, with just one extra column. It does not have the line of fate; instead, it directly shows what will happen within the set time frame, offering an easy narrative flow.

THE GAME OF HOPE, 6 × 6

The Game of Hope layout (six columns, six rows) is succinct and perfect for shorter time frames, allowing the reader to follow a narrative from start to finish. The first card in the Game of Hope tableau is the beginning of the set time frame, while the final card exiting the spread signifies the end of the time frame. Read in accordance with the techniques in this book, but also consider reading as a narrative flow from placement 1 to placement 36.

THE TAROT TABLEAU, 9 × 8 + 6

If you wanted to pull a full Tarot tableau, you would lay out in the 9 × 8 + 6 format. The houses would begin with the Majors and then follow through the suits (Wands, Cups, Swords, Pentacles). This is the largest of spreads and not for the faint of heart. It contains the full story of the Tarot deck and your querent's life—no stone left unturned. Longer time frames and major life events are highlighted, but it can be rather lengthy.

THE TAROT SUITS TABLEAU, 10 × 4

In the 10 × 4 layout, each row contains the suit houses from Ace through Ten. This is great for understanding exactly what is happening within the querent's daily life and how their four life areas are intertwined. It's also perfect for interpersonal relationships and understanding what is troublesome in each life area.

How to Choose a Significator

The significator is the card you choose to represent your querent in the spread—only Kings and Queens may play this role. If your querent is female and presented to you as the Queen of Swords, the partner card would be the King of Swords. Choosing a significator (King or Queen) to represent your querent does not have to be difficult. The most effective way is to reflect on the theme of the reading and choose the most appropriate. For example, if your querent were involved in a legal situation, you may choose the King or Queen of Swords to represent the attitude they will need to forge forward.

Rule of Thumb:

Practical   King or Queen of Pentacles

Emotional   King or Queen of Cups

Action   King or Queen of Swords

Motivation King or Queen of Wands

Remember: The person's significator dictates the direction of the tableau reading, cards ahead of the significator's gaze are considered to be "auspicious," and the cards behind the significators gaze are considered to be "inauspicious" (see more in advanced techniques on page 87).

The person's significator in a same-sex relationship remains the card that best represents the querent. The partner card will be either a Queen (for female same-sex relationships) or King (for male same-sex relationships); however, a King or Queen must be chosen that can look eye to eye with the querent's card. For example, if the King of Wands is chosen as the querent's significator, either the King of Cups or King of Pentacles must be chosen for the partner (*see directions below*).

Interpersonal Relationships

The Court cards will explain interpersonal relationships within the querent's life. Their placement in the spread will confirm whether connections are strong or troublesome.

Rule of Thumb:

Court cards facing one another in a spread will have a good relationship.

Court cards sitting back to back will show disharmony.

Court cards from the same suit will show people who belong together (e.g., family).

The directional cues can help us easily identify who we are getting along well with (facing one another) versus who we will have an issue with (sitting back to back).

Strong Relationship	Difficult Relationship

And this leads us directly to certain Court cards that can NEVER see eye to eye!

This does not mean that these two cannot work together on the same team; it is just not a close relationship status. They should not be chosen as significators for female partners (or similarly, Kings looking the same way should not be chosen for male partners).

Building a Narrative

The tableau affords a narrative storytelling experience; we can describe the querent's life and how it will unfold in the set time frame (the recommended time frame is one year). To read narratively, we need to understand how the cards interact with each other.

HORIZONTAL INTERACTION

The cards build on each other's meanings one by one to construct a storyline. The first card in your horizontal line will set the scene (or begin the sentence), and each card following explains the situation a little further.

Example for a relationship reading with no Significator:

Tower begins the interpretation with chaos.

Four of Cups explains what happens amid that chaos.

Nine of Pentacles explains what happens thereafter.

The querent's relationship is in crisis (Tower); she really cannot be bothered with all the drama (Four of Cups), so she moves into singledom and enjoys herself (Nine of Pentacles).

Each step along a horizontal line will add more interpretation.

Remember: The person's significator card will determine the direction in which we read. If a King or Queen is within your line of narrative, you will consider the cards behind their back to be troublesome and the cards ahead to be an easy route.

Inauspicious   Auspicious

We would read the above image as follows:

Cards 1, 2: Inauspicious meaning

Cards 4, 5: Auspicious meaning

Auspicious   Inauspicious

For the left-facing significator above, we would read as follows:

Card 1: Inauspicious meaning

Cards 3, 4, 5: Auspicious meaning

Here is an example of horizontal interaction with a right-facing significator (the King of Pentacles) card present:

Inauspicious   Auspicious

The querent is struggling to manage their workload (Two of Pentacles, inauspicious), but they are focused on expanding their career (Three of Wands). This works very well for the querent, and they feel that they are finally recognized in their position (Six of Wands) and can transition forward (Six of Swords) into their perfect role (Ten of Pentacles).

Each step along a horizontal line will add more interpretation:

Auspicious   Inauspicious

The significator card faces left in the image above. She is struggling to get to grips with her career status (Ten of Pentacles, inauspicious), and she keeps focusing on what she is doing wrong within it (the Six of Swords heading backward into the Queen and the Ten of Pentacles, inauspiciously). She is expecting success to knock on her doorstep (Six of Wands facing toward the Queen), but she must learn to look ahead with foresight and balance her future workload to bring this forth (Three of Wands and Two of Pentacles).

In a tableau, the cards weigh down in significance from the top to bottom. This means that the cards landing above your significator, or line of sight (see page 94), will impose their influence on the situations we are interpreting. Whilst we view the horizontal line as the storyline, we view the cards falling above and below as influencing that situation. Life is full of twists and turns—some situations influence others, and our thoughts and behaviors influence our actions. It is all shown in the vertical interactions within a spread. We can enhance our readings further by considering the cards above to be an external influence on the situation, while the cards below show how our own behavior affects the situation.

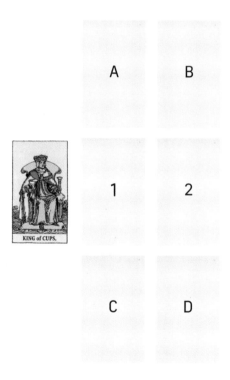

Cards 1 and 2 (*left*) show our querent's direct line of sight (see page 94); this is the row in which your significator sits and shows direct actions/happenings. The cards above and below (A, B, C, D) influence this baseline situation. That is to say:

Card 1 shows the beginning of the situation.

Cards A and C explain what is influencing this situation further.

Then Card 2 occurs (explained further by cards B and D).

Advanced Tableau Techniques

Tableau Advanced
TECHNIQUE 1: AUSPICIOUS VERSUS INAUSPICIOUS

Find your significator card in the tableau and note its position. The tableau reading begins by choosing the appropriate King or Queen for the querent and noting the direction of the significator's gaze. The cards ahead form an auspicious narrative (fortunate, easy), and the cards behind the significator's back form the inauspicious narrative (unfortunate, difficult).

Rule of Thumb for Significator Placement:

- The higher in the spread, the more control your querent has of their situation (active position).

- The lower in the spread, the more the situation is out of control (inactive position).

- Many cards ahead (auspicious placement) show a fortunate time frame.

- Many cards behind (inauspicious placement) highlight a difficult situation.

Best
(Right facing)

Best
(Left facing)

Worst
(Left facing)

Worst
(Right facing)

TECHNIQUE 2: INTERPERSONAL RELATIONSHIPS

In addition to the significators that you have chosen for your querent and their partner, other people will attend your tableau. Their placement, in conjunction with the significators, will explain the nature of each relationship. Note any additional people within the spread—who they could possibly be (on the basis of the suit and placement)—and explain how their placement describes their relationship with the querent. Are they aspected positively or negatively?

All cards within a tableau interact with the neighboring cards; the significator for your querent is no exception, and the surrounding cards will begin your narrative.

Right Facing				Left Facing		
A	1	B		B	1	A
4		2		2		4
C	3	D		D	3	C

Placements:

1 The thoughts of the querent

A Inauspicious meaning affecting thoughts (card 1) and difficulties (card 4)

2 The focus of the querent

B Auspicious meaning affecting thoughts (card 1) and focus (card 2)

3 The feelings of the querent

C The most inauspicious placement shows the querent's problems (affects cards 3 and 4).

4 The difficulties in the situation

D Auspicious meanings affecting cards 2 and 3

Note: This can also be completed for any other Kings and Queens within the spread to confirm their roles within the given time frame.

TECHNIQUE 4: ATTENDANCE

The general "mood" of a tableau is the first telltale sign of the direction of the narrative. If you think about life in general, we have times when everything is hunky-dory, run of the mill, and status quo. Then there are years filled with amazing and uplifting major events, such as marriage or moving to a new home. On the other hand, there are years when troubling situations arise, from legal matters to financial issues on the horizon. Then there are years that incorporate it all—a rollercoaster of a time. By thinking of life in this way (i.e., really considering the kinds of years we have experienced) and applying it to the tableau, you will find that it helps navigate the direction of the narrative fluidly.

When your Grand Tableau is in front of you, consider the following:

- How many Majors are attending?

- Is there a dominant suit (i.e., more cards in one suit than others)?

- Is there a "missing suit" (i.e., one suit does not attend)?

- What "kind" of suits are attending (i.e., troublesome or easy cards)?

- Is there a grouping of suits in numbers (i.e., all fours from the deck)?

MAJOR ATTENDANCE

The number of Majors attending will determine the significance of the life events shown. The more Majors that present in a spread, the more significant the situation. A typical, run-of-the-mill year with no major occurrences (marriage, career advancement, death, etc.) will appear as a tableau with only a few Majors present. Each additional Major raises the significance of the year shown. It is important to understand which Majors attend and whether they share a commonality that sows a thread of narrative between them. (For example, Death, the World, and the Wheel of Fortune suggest completion and cycles, while the Emperor, Justice, and Judgment discuss legalities.) Look to the Majors attending to understand what life areas or events are being highlighted, and use the "amplifies" section of each meaning to interpret the significance shown.

Attendance follows systems such as Skat and Playing-Cards Cartomancy to highlight the "dominance" of life theme. The two most dominant suits confirm the theme of the reading. For example, Wands and Pentacles highlight creative careers, while Cups and Wands show passionate relationships.

Suit Attendance

WANDS

When many Wands attend, it is a year of energy, gearing up, and planning followed by setting creative projects alight. This can show a real action year as far as work is concerned, but also indicates increased action for other themed readings too. Look to the second dominant suit to understand what the Wands are mixing with to confirm the life area that is seeing so much action!

CUPS

We know that the Cups are an emotional bunch, which speak of everything from union to a happily ever after. If lots of Cups attend, it is an emotional year, but this heightened emotionality does not necessarily mean it is a year for love and relationships (in fact, your second-highest suit will confirm what kind of life area is being affected). What it *does* mean is that the client's emotional status is being shown above all.

SWORDS

Most readers focus on the intellectual meanings behind the Swords suit, but it is also important to remember that they are a suit of active change, for better or for worse, and our conscious suit where we make our intentional decisions about life. The Swords suit is also our troublesome suit, full of many challenging cards. When you have a majority of Swords in a reading, there will be troubles and changes ahead—a rocky road moving forward.

PENTACLES

The mood of the tableau with many Pentacles is totally practical—focus on working hard to achieve what we wish to achieve! Finances, work, and practical matters all come to the forefront with our Pentacles, and we can look to the second-highest suit attending to see how this focus on the practical is manifesting throughout the year.

Note: The absence of any one suit will also provide you with additional interpretation; namely, that the suit's essence will be missing from the time frame. This is particularly noteworthy if we have a themed reading—for example, love—yet, no Cups attend, highlighting the lack of emotional balance within the period.

NUMBER ATTENDANCE

Within the section on pips' meanings, we discussed understanding the numbers one to ten and applied them within the core essence meaning of the cards. Pay attention, and you may see a cluster of cards with the same number presenting together; this will bring in the power of that number to the interpretation.

1   Individuality, new beginnings

2   Duality, polarity

3   Trinity, connections

4   Earthly, practical, stable

5   External influence, individualism in the face of adversity

6   Move away from adversity; self-acceptance

7   Karmic lessons, reactions

8   Transformation, actions

9   Payback, give and take

10 Manifestation, completion

CLUSTER ATTENDANCE

"Clusters" are a group of cards connected together to confirm a narrative. They share a commonality that weaves the interpretation into a theme. As you become proficient in reading tableaus, you will notice that some cards will "hang out together" when a certain theme is presented—make a note of these and create your own list of clusters for possible eventualities.

It is important to understand your Tarot deck and the intricacies of the situation you are reading for before you lay a tableau. Having a "perfect complement" of clusters would mean that all the cards you expect to show for a particular event land within the tableau, confirming that the situation will indeed happen. For example, if you have a client who would like to see a marriage proposal within their year ahead, it is important to make a mental note of cards that would signify marriage (the Lovers, Four of Wands, Two of Cups, Ten of Cups, the Hierophant, etc.), and also note the cards that would signify a proposal (Page of Cups, Ace of Cups, Six of Cups, etc.). If they all fall together within your spread, then you have your confirmation that a marriage proposal will occur, with no doubt in your mind. If, however, the "perfect cluster" does not fall within the spread, look to see which components do and what this confirms about the situation.

On page 120, you will find a list of example clusters.

MOVEMENT

The movement cards within your tableau will add to every step of your interpretation. Many movement cards clustering in the spread will show high action and highly dynamic situations; they will also highlight physical movement, such as going on holiday or moving to a new home. Find your movement cards within the spread and determine what their directional cues add to the interpretation. See the example reading on page 128.

TECHNIQUE 5: KNIGHTS & PAGES

The Knights can help with context in a tableau—by understanding what action is incoming or taken by the querent, we can understand how situations will evolve. Find the Knights within your tableau and explain the start of the action (the card behind the Knight) and how it will impact the querent's life (the card ahead of the Knight).

The Pages highlight incoming or outgoing communication. This is pertinent in many situations and allows the querent to understand what will be arriving and how it will affect their lives. The card behind the Page explains the source of the communication, and the card ahead of the Page will show what impact that news will have. See page 128 for an example.

TECHNIQUE 6: THE DIRECT LINE OF SIGHT

The most important narrative within the tableau, the "direct line of sight," is the row in which your significator sits, and shows the direct action and occurrences within your time frame. It is a narrative that quite simply explains what will happen. The direct line of sight is read in the direction of your significator, beginning with the first card in the row (*see the image below*).

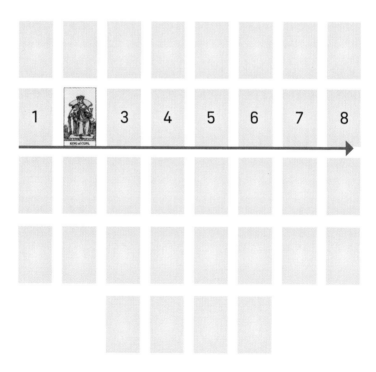

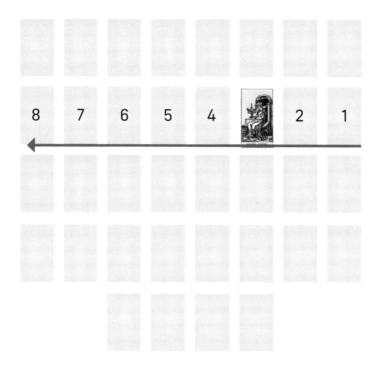

We always begin our narrative with the most difficult of situations (behind the significator's back) and then transition into the more auspicious aspects, creating a fluid interpretation. In the example image above, the Queen of Cups has two cards behind her back in an inauspicious position; cards 1 and 2 begin our narrative. String your sentences together as you move from card 1 through to card 8 in a comprehensive storyline.

See example on page 129.

For advanced readers: At each step of the narration, you may add in the cards above and below to understand the horizontal and vertical influences (see pages 83–86).

TECHNIQUE 7: THE CARTOMANTIC APPROACH

The Cartomantic Approach adds another layer to your interpretations, filling in the missing information and substantiating your predictions. We have a wealth of techniques available—from knighting to mirroring—that we can apply one by one until we feel we have explored all the information provided.

KNIGHTING

The role of knighting is to discover what strategies are playing a role in the situation. Much like the movements in chess, knighting requires the reader to move in an L shape. Knighting represents strategy and how we surprise our opponent with a well-thought-out move. It is the only chess piece that can jump over others and often takes a seemingly random route, strategically cherry-picking its spot. When we knight with our cards, we are doing exactly that: we are strategically seeing the situation from a different perspective—seeing the pattern or logic within the random, the organized within the seemingly disorganized. It's often likened to seeing the underbelly of a situation for what it really is.

The movement is as follows:

- Two steps in one direction, then one step at 90 degrees, or
- One step in one direction, then two steps at 90 degrees

We will not have a full complement of knighting moves every time we read; the placement of the significator will determine how much knighting information is available.

The cards available in a knighted position will explain more about the querent's position in the storyline you have narrated through the previous techniques. Add the knighted cards behind the significator (inauspicious placement) to explain negative strategies that are influencing the situation, and the knighted cards ahead of the significator (auspicious placement) to understand what strategies are benefiting the querent.

Simply work through the knighted cards, adding them into your current storyline to explain what strategies are at play. It is not important which knighted cards you read first, so long as you understand their role in an inauspicious versus auspicious placement. See example on page 132.

DIAGONALS

The diagonal influences flowing outward from your significator will confirm dynamic influences within the scenario. These influences reveal which parts of the situation are progressing in an auspicious or inauspicious manner. The significator card always acts as the focal point of our attention, and we read each diagonal within the context of our interpretation up to this point. Below is an example of diagonal placement:

Negative dynamic influences (cards 1 & 2)
Shows what is negatively impacting the situation

Negative dynamic actions (card 5)
Highlights the biggest failings in the situation

Positive dynamic influences (cards 3 & 4)
Explains the positive influences on the situation

Positive dynamic action (cards 6 & 7)
Best advice on how to act moving forward

In your narrative, include how the cards within the diagonal dynamic influence placement affect the storyline you have built to date.

See example on page 132.

Knighting

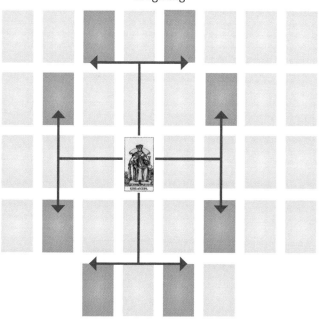

Diagonals

Mirroring allows the reader to see a reflection of the situation and how it evolves—or where it began! Choose a card within the spread to gain more information about how it will develop, or where it came from! Mirroring involves imagining the tableau folded into four halves, divided along the horizontal and vertical center. If you are reading with a tableau that has a "line of fate" (see page 80), simply ignore the bottom line in your mirroring process (*see image*).

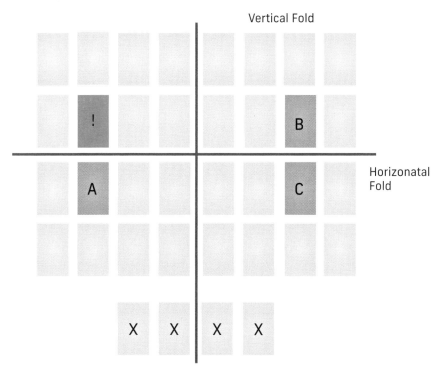

The pink card in this illustration is the card that you would like to clarify.

The purple cards are the mirrored cards.

Pink: Card of interest

A: Status of the situation right now

B: Future development of that situation

C: Future status of that situation

Note: If your card of interest is on the right-hand side of the spread (e.g., placement B above), the mirrored cards to the left will show how that situation begins.

TECHNIQUE 8:
THE MASTER METHOD: THE HOUSES

"Houses" are another term for placements within a spread. A house will hold a core life theme that applies to your querent's question, and the card that lands within a house will show the status of the life theme within the set time frame. For example, if we have a house that is labeled "Love," the card that lands within it will explain how the querent's love life will unfold. Note that if you choose a themed reading (such as career or finances), the house will relate to the chosen theme (the Love house then becomes how much the querent will love their career or finances!). Always refer back to the reading's theme when understanding house placements.

The image below shows the houses in the 8 × 4 + 4 and 9 × 4 layouts. If you complete a different-sized tableau, apply the houses in sequence (house 1 to 36) in your chosen configuration:

The Grand Tableau, 8 × 4 + 4

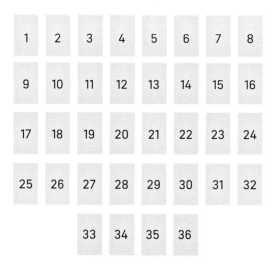

Tableau, 9 × 4

1	2	3	4	5	6	7	8	9
10	11	12	13	14	15	16	17	18
19	20	21	22	23	24	25	26	27
28	29	30	31	32	33	34	35	36

HOUSE		ESSENCE
1	Projects	Projects including hobbies and sideline jobs
2	Satisfaction	Measure the levels of the querent's satisfaction.
3	Success	Measure the querent's success.
4	Hope	Hopeful situation
5	Chance	How much luck or what will be lucky
6	Wishes	Desires and wants for the time frame
7	Injustice	This will work against the querent.
8	Ingratitude	What the querent does not appreciate
9	Association	Describes associations from friends to businesses
10	Loss	Losses and forfeiture
11	Trouble	Issues and problems
12	State or Condition	State of the querent's life in the time frame
13	Joy	Elation, joy
14	Love	Love, connections
15	Prosperity	Abundant, plentiful, overflowing
16	Marriage	Relationship status

HOUSE	ESSENCE (continued)
17 Sorrow/Affliction	Sorrow, sadness, unpleasant events
18 Pleasure	Fun, games, enjoyment
19 Inheritance/Property	Incoming payments that are owed to the querent
20 Fraud/Deceit	Betrayal, deceit, hidden information
21 Rivals	Competition, enemies, anything working against the querent
22 Gift	Incoming gifts, surprises
23 Lover	The status of their lover
24 Advancement	Growth, expansion, career advancement
25 Kindness	Kindness, affection
26 Enterprise	Business, commerce, trade
27 Changes	Changes, relocations, movement
28 The End (of Life)	Endings, death
29 Reward	Honor, merits, promotion
30 Misfortune/Disgrace	Adversity, accidents, disrepute
31 Happiness	Happiness, contentment
32 Money/Fortune	Financial status
33 Indifference	Ignorance, lack of interest
34 Favor	What will be auspicious
35 Ambition	Will ambitions be met, or in what area will they be ambitious?
36 Ill Health	Illness, bad health, unhealthful situations

It is not essential to read every house within a reading; utilize the houses when you would like to gain more knowledge, or choose the houses pertaining to your querent's question. For example, if reading about a relationship, we would check houses 14, 16, 23, and any others to gain understanding about the specific aspect of the relationship we are examining.

See page 134, for example.

TECHNIQUE 9: THE LINE OF FATE

The "line of fate" is a final line at the bottom of your tableau, consisting of four cards. Not every tableau layout includes the line of fate—some tableaus create a perfect rectangle. The line of fate is a welcome addition when you want additional information pertaining to the theme of choice for the querent. The line can be interpreted as "The querent would like this to happen, but it will not happen in the set time frame" or "This will happen whether the querent likes it or not!" What matters is to set your intention for your line of fate before beginning the reading.

You choose the intention for your line of fate:

Either   "This will happen within the time frame for sure."

Or   "This will NOT happen within the time frame."

If you would like to know whether a querent can expect a house move within the set time frame, set the intention that the line of fate "will not happen within the time frame." Then, when cards detailing movement or sale of house show up in the line of fate, you know for sure that the answer is "no" within the given time frame.

If you wish to lay a general tableau for a year ahead, set the intention for the line of fate to detail "what will happen for sure." This way, you will understand what fated events are due to enter the querent's life.

See example on page 135.

TECHNIQUE 10: TIMING

The most significant prediction a tableau can offer the reader is the ability to time a situation and predict events on a day-by-day or month-by-month basis. Each column of the tableau represents a time frame within the spread. When practicing, it is useful to create a simple timeline for your readings to understand the flow of time. I suggest that each column represents a time frame (e.g., one day, one week, one month) to ensure clarity and prevent confusion within the columns.

Remember:

- Your time frame begins behind your significator's back.

- If you have a right-facing Court card, your first time period will be on the left-hand column.

- If you have a left-facing Court card, your first time period will be on the right-hand column.

- Column 1 represents the first time period (one day, one week, one month).

- Column 8 represents the end of the time frame (eighth day, eighth week, eighth month).

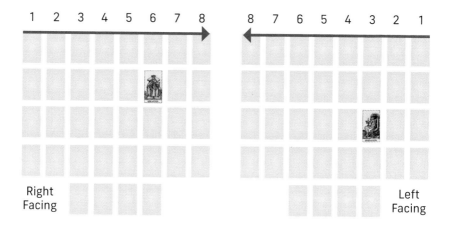

We employ the full spectrum of interpretation techniques to cover every card within the tableau; it may seem overwhelming at first, but remember:

- The line of sight (the row the significator sits in) shows direct actions and occurrences.

- The cards above the line of sight explain any influences that can be seen.

- The cards below the line of sight highlight any underlying storyline.

In this vein, if we take column 1 as our first time period, we read the card sitting in the line of sight as a situation unfolding, and proceed to explain the cards above and below pertaining to that time period and situation.

See example on page 136.

Alternative Tableau Spreads

Nine-Card Tableau

The Nine-Card Tableau is a quick and effective way to navigate any situation—a spread that can answer any complex situation in a short, sharp, and succinct manner. It is important, as with all tableaus, to note whether a person's significator lands in the spread. This will change your Nine-Card Tableau from an inactive situation to an active one, one in which the querent is being directly affected (for better or worse) by the surrounding cards.

- Shuffle your Tarot deck.
- Ask your question.
- Set your intention to lay a nine-card box.
- Lay the cards in three rows of three cards.

NINE-CARD TABLEAU WITH A PERSON'S SIGNIFICATOR

The Nine-Card Tableau with a King or Queen attending depicts an active situation for the person shown. In this case, we automatically shift our reading techniques to perform the "Significator Square" placements regarding auspicious versus inauspicious information (see page 89). The cards behind the significator show the inauspicious aspects, and cards ahead of the significator reveal the auspicious interpretation (within the directional gaze of the significator). As in the larger tableaus, the position of the significator is important: their placement high in the spread indicates levels of control, while placement in the bottom row suggests being totally out of control. In addition, the column in which the significator lands will determine the difficulty of the situation for the querent (see image below, highlighting the inauspicious cards behind the significator).

The Queen of Cups in the following image lands in column 3 (reading right to left due to significator facing left). The two columns behind her back have inauspicious meanings. She does not have an auspicious line, showing a very difficult situation to overcome.

3   2   1

Card above Significator	Thoughts
Card below Significator	Feelings
Cards behind Significator	Inauspicious meanings
Cards ahead of Significator	Auspicious meanings

NOTE: You will not always have a full complement of placements. If the significator lands at the top or the bottom of the spread, one or more placements will be missing. This absence provides additional information to the reader. For example, if the "Thoughts" placement is missing, it highlights that this is a time for action, not consideration. Similarly, if the "Feelings" placement is missing, it is not the time to be led by intuition—more conscious decision-making needs to occur!

- Begin by explaining the thoughts (card above) and feelings (card below) of the querent.

- Read the line of sight for the querent: interpret the cards in the same row as the significator, moving from inauspicious to auspicious, as a narrative.

- Read the inauspicious column(s).
- Read the auspicious column(s).

NINE-CARD TABLEAU WITHOUT A PERSON'S SIGNIFICATOR

The Nine-Card Tableau with no King or Queen attending shows a passive situation in the querent's life, or one that happens without their input. It is read as follows:

Center:	Card 5, the answer to the question (the main focus of the reading)
Rows:	Narratively read through cards 1 to 9 in a storytelling fashion
Columns:	Read each column from top to bottom narratively.

By reading each card with horizontal and vertical interactions, the reader thoroughly covers the answer to the question asked.

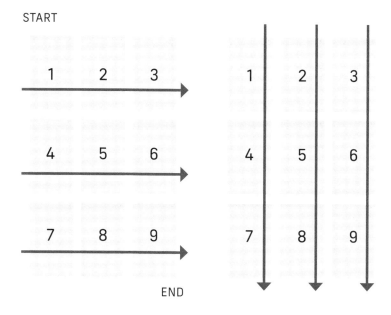

START

1	2	3
4	5	6
7	8	9

END

107

The Mini Tableau

Small but mighty, the Mini Tableau affords the reader the opportunity to employ tableau techniques in a compact format. This serves as the perfect step into larger spreads, allowing the reader to build upon the interactions therein. This spread highlights interpersonal relationships and delves deeply into various situations. The Mini Tableau consists of fourteen cards laid out as per the image below:

- Think of your question.
- Set your intention to perform a Mini Tableau.
- Set your significator card for the querent aside.
- Shuffle your deck and count the top thirteen cards.
- Shuffle the significator cards into the thirteen top cards.
- Lay the Mini Tableau.

Once you have your tableau in front of you, work through the tableau techniques to interpret.

The Fool's Journey Tableau

The Fool's Journey provides the backdrop to the Major Arcana Tableau and is read in conjunction with the cards presented. Each Major Arcana card becomes a house (or placement) within the spread, enabling the reader to follow a client's future storyline. Consider the Major Arcana cards (0–XXII) to denote a step further in our own path of life, with lessons that we learn along the way. The cards that fall onto this journey explain how each step will present in the year ahead. Simply employ the Tarot Tableau techniques in conjunction with the Fool's Journey houses (*below*).

Major Arcana Tarot Tableau Layout:

HOUSE/PLACEMENT MEANINGS:

0	Fool	The focus of the reading—what future is the querent walking into?
I	Magician	What new skill set will the querent need?
II	High Priestess	What universal knowledge will the querent find?
III	The Empress	What will the querent be nurturing in the time frame?
IV	The Emperor	What will require control?
V	The Hierophant	What will require structure?
VI	The Lovers	What connections will the querent experience?
VII	The Chariot	What movement can be seen?
VIII	Strength	What will need strength?
IX	The Hermit	What will require a step back into self?
X	The Wheel of Fortune	What changes are going to happen?
XI	Justice	What decisions are being made (for or against us)?
XII	The Hanged Man	What sacrifice or perspective is needed?
XIII	Death	What will end?
XIV	Temperance	What needs molding?
XV	The Devil	What temptations are foreseen?
XVI	The Tower	What chaos will ensue?
XVII	The Star	What direction will be fortunate?
XVIII	The Moon	What is not known?
XIX	The Sun	What will be positive?
XX	Judgment	What evaluation is needed?
XXI	The World	What will be completed within the time frame?

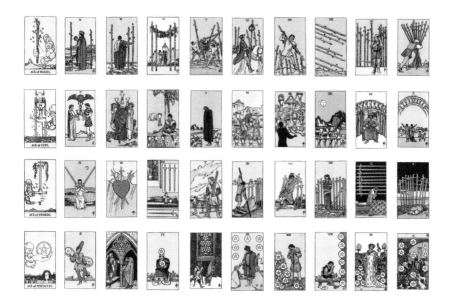

The Tarot Suits Tableau: 10 × 4

The Tarot Suits Tableau, as shown in the image above, uses the suit houses as its base. Cards are laid in four rows of ten, with each row representing the suit's movement from the Ace through to the Ten. This tableau is designed for daily occurrences and delves into the mundane aspects of life. It is important to note how many of the cards land within their own suit row, and to explain the meaning of each card within the house in which it sits.

For example, when the Ten of Wands falls in the house of Three of Cups, it suggests that the querent is finding socializing to be hard work or they just have too many invites on their calendar!

You can easily follow this spread by using two decks:

Deck 1   Lay the suits in the above sequence (these are your "houses").

Deck 2   Shuffle and lay cards on top of the houses (including your chosen significator).

Begin with the suit of Wands houses (top row) and explain each card landing in each house. For example, the Nine of Pentacles lands in the house of the

Two of Wands, explaining that rewards can be expected if the querent has planned well. As you walk through each row, tell the story of each suit in conjunction with the cards landing within them. Don't forget to add tableau techniques!

The Fan: 5 + 3

The Fan layout is not technically a tableau, but it is read in accordance with the storytelling-narrative flow that we are accustomed to. The Fan was commonly used in nineteenth-century Europe, when fortune-telling was outlawed, allowing the reader to covertly interpret whilst giving the impression that a card game was being played. The Fan can be read singularly, for our own fortunes, or as a two-player reading session (*see below*).

Two-Player Fan Layout Instructions:

- **Shuffle your deck** and set your intention to perform a fan reading.
- **Set aside** the significator card for your querent. (optional)
- **Take fifteen cards** from the top of the deck.
- **Shuffle the significator** into the fifteen cards (you now have sixteen cards). (optional)
- **Deal the cards** between you and your querent.
- **Hold your cards** in your hand, with cards 1 to 5 at the top (*see image*) and cards 6 to 8 at the bottom.
- **Explain to your querent** how to hold their cards the same as you.

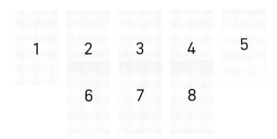

HOW TO READ THE FAN LAYOUT:

Reader's Cards	The Statements
1–5	= the answer to the question.
6–7	= the issues within the situation.
8	= the outcome.

Querent's Cards	The Responses
1–5	= the querent's actions and reactions to the reader's card.
6–7	= how the querent will overcome obstacles.
8	= the outcome.

The reader and querent take turns placing cards one at a time on the table, similar to a game of "Snap."

Example Reading:

The querent is female and would like to know what her chances of career progression are within the coming year.

NOTE: It is the reader who interprets both the statement and the answer.

READER LAYS CARD 1: The Chariot
The Statement: A great card to start the narration, confirming that there will be successes and drive within the set time frame.

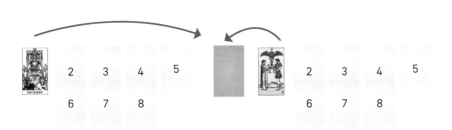

QUERENT LAYS CARD 1: Two of Cups
The Answer: This card highlights that she will be working on close collaborations and finding the right balance for her.

READER LAYS CARD 2: Five of Pentacle
The Statement: Whilst you are focusing on finding the right collaborations, it is important not to ignore lesser offerings.

QUERENT LAYS CARD 2: Five of Wands
The Answer: That is all good and well, but it leads to a conflict in what I really want to do.

READER LAYS CARD 3: Seven of Cups
The Statement: Yes, but if you focus on the lesser offerings (i.e., those that are not perfect), it will lead to more options being available.

QUERENT LAYS CARD 3: Two of Swords
The Answer: I understand, but I struggle to make decisions when there are too many options.

READER LAYS CARD 4: The Emperor
The Statement: It may be difficult to make decisions, but it is time to take control of the situation.

QUERENT LAYS CARD 4: Four of Pentacles
The Answer: I tend to go with what I know rather than the unknown.

Reader lays card 5: Six of Swords

The Statement: If you do transition and take control, you will see your career advancing.

QUERENT LAYS CARD 5: The Tower
The Answer: I will break down my comfort zone and break down that which is not serving me.

READER LAYS CARD 6: Three of Pentacles
The Statement: We are working on your problems now, and we can see it is difficult for you to work as a team.

QUERENT LAYS CARD 6: King of Pentacles
The Answer: Yes, I tend to take control of team situations rather than being part of the team.

READER LAYS CARD 7: Nine of Pentacles
The Statement: You are a little too independent in that respect, and although it does serve you well to be self-sufficient, there are times when you should think less singularly.

Querent lays card 7: Eight of Cups

The Answer: That will be a difficult trait to move away from.

Reader lays card 8: Six of Wands

The Statement: If you can overcome your teamwork issues and open yourself to all possibilities (i.e., do not shrug off the lesser offerings), you will find the success you seek.

QUERENT LAYS CARD 8: The Star
The Answer: I will focus on this direction and set my manifestation in motion.

Quick Glance

Major Arcana Quick Glance

No.	Card	Auspicious	Inauspicious	Type
0	The Fool	Spontaneity	Folly	Directional
1	The Magician	Skill	Manipulation	Highlight
II	The High Priestess	Intuition	Secrets	Stationary
III	The Empress	Nurture	Overbearing	Directional
IV	The Emperor	Authority	Domineering	Stationary
V	The Hierophant	Tradition	Dogmatic	Stationary
VI	The Lovers	Love	Disharmony	Highlight
VII	The Chariot	Drive	Lack of direction	Highlight
VIII	Strength	Fortitude	Assertion	Directional
IX	The Hermit	Circumspection	Withdrawal	Directional
X	The Wheel of Fortune	Fortune	Misfortune	Stationary
XI	Justice	Equality	Unfairness	Stationary
XII	The Hanged Man	Perspective	Stasis	Highlight
XIII	Death	Ending	Death	Directional
XIV	Temperance	Balance	Instability	Highlight
XV	The Devil	Temptation	Compulsion	Highlight
XVI	The Tower	Chaos	Destruction	Highlight

XVII	The Star	Hope	False hope	Stationary
XVIII	The Moon	Deception	Fraud	Stationary
XIX	The Sun	Energetic	Toxic positivity	Stationary
XX	Judgment	Evaluation	Negative outcome	Stationary
XXI	The World	Completion	Emptiness	Stationary

Court Cards Quick Glance

Card	Suit	Auspicious	Inauspicious	Direction
Page	Wands	Inspired	Distracted	Right
Page	Cups	Idyllic	Immature	Left
Page	Swords	Witty	Gossipy	Left
Page	Pentacles	Diligent	Irresponsible	Right
Knight	Wands	Enthusiasm	Volatile	Left
Knight	Cups	Charming	Vain	Right
Knight	Swords	Assertive	Rude	Left
Knight	Pentacles	Practical	Workaholic	Right
Queen	Wands	Confident	Challenging	Right
Queen	Cups	Ally	Needy	Left
Queen	Swords	Objective	Bitter	Right
Queen	Pentacles	Industrious	Materialistic	Left
King	Wands	Motivating	Forceful	Left
King	Cups	Advisor	Cold	Right
King	Swords	Professional	Malicious	Left
King	Pentacles	Secure	Possessive	Right

The Pips Quick Glance

No.	Suit	Auspicious	Inauspicious	Movement
Ace	Wands	New inspiration	Recklessness	No
Ace	Cups	New emotions	Flaky	No
Ace	Swords	New ideas	The truth	No
Ace	Pentacles	An opportunity	Meager offers	No
2	Wands	Planning	Overanalyzing	No
2	Cups	Partnership	Separation	No
2	Swords	Difficult decisions	Stalemate	No
2	Pentacles	Multitasking	Unorganized	No
3	Wands	Progress	Obstacles	No
3	Cups	Celebration	Excess	No
3	Swords	Grief	Devastation	No
3	Pentacles	Teamwork	Ineffective team	No
4	Wands	Stability	Instability	No
4	Cups	Apathy	Indifference	No
4	Swords	Rest	Burnout	No
4	Pentacles	Protecting investments	Possessiveness	No
5	Wands	Competition	Rivalry	No
5	Cups	Disappointment	Grief	No
5	Swords	Conflict	Hostility	No
5	Pentacles	Hardship	Insolvency	Right

6	Wands	Success	Ill-gained success	Right
6	Cups	Memories	Childish	No
6	Swords	Transition	Fleeing	Right
6	Pentacles	Sharing	Oversharing	No
7	Wands	Upper hand	Interference	Below
7	Cups	Opportunities	Confusion	No
7	Swords	Deception	Vengeance	Left
7	Pentacles	Patience	Setbacks	No
8	Wands	Motion	Hasty	Right
8	Cups	Leaving	Abandonment	Right
8	Swords	Restriction	Paralysis	No
8	Pentacles	Practice	Lack of attention	No
9	Wands	Persistence	Stubbornness	No
9	Cups	Satisfaction	Egotistical	No
9	Swords	Anxiety	Misery	No
9	Pentacles	Attainment	Singledom	No
10	Wands	Burden	Pressure	Right
10	Cups	Happiness	Disharmony	No
10	Swords	Pain	Disaster	No
10	Pentacles	Stability	Fleeting success	No

Example Clusters

The following list of clusters is by no means exhaustive; it provides an indication of possible interpretations that can be applied to the question of your reading. These interpretations are valid only if the clusters fall close together and near the person's significator.

Theme	Major	Minors
Love	The Lovers	Ace of Cups
		Two of Cups
		Page of Cups
Work	The Emperor	Three of Pentacles
		Seven of Pentacles
		Eight of Pentacles
Cheating	The Devil	Three of Cups
	The Moon	Three of Pentacles
	The Lovers (inauspicious)	Six of Pentacles
		Nine of Pentacles
		Page of Wands
		Page of Cups
Marriage	The Lovers	Two of Cups
	The Hierophant	Four of Wands
		Ten of Cups
		Ten of Pentacles

Divorce	The Lovers (inauspicious)	Two of Cups (inauspicious)
	The Tower	Three of Swords
	Death	Eight of Cups
	Justice	
Promotion	The Chariot	Three of Wands
	The Emperor	Three of Cups
	The Star	Six of Wands
		Ten of Pentacles
Job Opportunities	The Chariot	Ace of Pentacles
	The Lovers	Ace of Wands
	The Star	Six of Wands
		Six of Pentacles
		Seven of Cups
		Page of Pentacles
		Knight of Pentacles

Tarot Tableau Example Reading

The reading below is for a female querent (Queen of Cups) who would like to know the future of her marriage; her partner is male (King of Cups), and the couple have no children.

Technique 1: Auspicious versus Inauspicious Placement

The Queen of Cups (the querent) is seated toward the top of the tableau, with five columns of auspicious cards ahead of her. She is in a good position of control within the situation and will handle it with active participation, adopting a hands-on, "Let's do this" approach. Two columns of inauspicious cards sit behind her back, confirming that there will be issues to overcome (further steps will confirm more).

Technique 2: Interpersonal Relationships

The partner card (King of Cups) is position at the bottom of the spread, exiting the tableau. He has no active control and is weighed down by the circumstances. The couple sits back to back, suggesting discord within the relationship (further steps will confirm more).

Additionally, the King of Pentacles attends in an auspicious position, surrounded by knights. This indicates someone entering the querent's life (due to the number of knights), who will have a significant impact.

Technique 3: The Significator Square

Thoughts: Six of Swords

Focus: Ten of Wands

Difficulties: Two of Swords

Feelings: Ten of Swords

The querent is thinking it is time to move on (Six of Swords). She feels betrayed (Ten of Swords) and is struggling to make decisions (Two of Swords). All she can focus on is how badly it is affecting her (Ten of Wands).

She has been forced to make decisions about moving forward, which have been challenging (inauspicious column). She feels deep sadness at the ending, but it is time to take a step back, reevaluate, and look at how she can meet her responsibilities now. The Five of Pentacles under the Ten of Wands shows how she is struggling to meet responsibilities, but in an auspicious position, it indicates she will work through it!

In the following Partner Square, the partner card sits in the most inauspicious position within the tableau, and with no cards beneath, we see that his feelings do not factor into the situation—only his thoughts!

The partner is deeply hurt, and given its position exiting the spread, we can suggest he is on his way out (if not already gone). He has struggled with what he deems to be forceful manipulation (Strength + Magician) and has had enough (exiting the spread).

Interestingly, both person significator cards share the inauspicious line with Strength and the Magician, highlighting mistrust and possibly forceful and manipulative behavior that was unacceptable. With the cards sitting closest to the partner card and with the Two of Swords closest to the querent, we can suggest that the partner will employ devious and forceful tactics in the breakdown of the relationship, leading the querent to be forced to make difficult decisions.

This is a marriage in crisis, which leads us to the Major attendance!

THE KING OF PENTACLES SQUARE

Due to the theme being a relationship theme and a relationship in crisis, the King of Pentacles stands out as another prospect within the querent's life. We know this is not the partner (because the King of Cups is automatically the partner card), but he sits prominently within the spread, showing influence on the situation.

Thoughts: Knight of Pentacles

Focus: The Sun

Difficulties: Four of Wands

Feelings: Knight of Cups

The King of Pentacles is entering with plenty of action! He rides in excited (Knight of Cups below) and thinking he has an opportunity (Knight of Pentacles) to start with a brand-new love that is happy and evoking feelings of finding one's true self again (auspicious column). He does not come without

baggage; he too has walked away from a once-solid relationship (inauspicious), but he is ready to move on (knights showing the dynamic move).

By analyzing the positions of the above court cards and the squares around each, we can confirm that the querent will be leaving their current partner quite soon (who will be heartbroken but who does show manipulative force within the relationship) and that a new beau is on the horizon in the form of the King of Pentacles. He will ride in like her knight in shining armor and bring a positive attitude that is charming. She will love his dynamic energy, but will he knock her off her feet? Further steps will reveal this!

Technique 4: Attendance

MAJOR ATTENDANCE

We have five Majors attending the spread auspiciously:

XIV	The Devil
XVI	The Tower
XIX	The Sun
XVIII	The Moon
VI	The Lovers

In an auspicious position, we have some troublesome Majors, enough to confirm that our theme of relationships is going to be chaotic within the time frame. This indicates a significant relationship event that cannot be dismissed as simple arguments or a moment of dispute. This raises our level of reading from everyday occurrences and "run-of-the-mill" life to a serious relationship situation that could end in a breakup (but we will explore this further).

And two Majors attending inauspiciously:

| I | The Magician |
| VIII | Strength |

The Magician and Strength in an inauspicious position are a nasty combo! The Magician becomes skillful at manipulating situations to his advantage, and the Strength card becomes assertive and forceful in its application. If there were more evidence around (e.g., Three of Cups, Seven of Swords, Three of Pentacles, Page of Cups), we could suggest that the partner is cheating with these two

Majors attending. However, in the absence of substantiation, we understand that the partner has been domineering, manipulative, and possibly extremely passive-aggressive.

SUIT ATTENDANCE

Wands	5
Swords	9
Cups	10 (including significators)
Pentacles	5

The Swords and Cups hold the majority in this reading, indicating that the focus is not on financial or creative pursuits but rather on emotions and action. This aligns well with the storyline we have interpreted thus far.

NUMBER ATTENDANCE

There are a few repeating numbers within the spread. Most notably, we have the Two of Wands and Two of Cups together at the beginning of the spread (hanging around with two tens). This shows the duality of the situation between the querent and her partner, and how the culmination of this relationship (the tens) is enabling the querent to see her place clearly as an individual within a couple (the twos).

Additionally, the Four of Swords, Four of Wands, and Four of Cups highlight that the querent's relationship status will move into a much more stable period within the set time frame.

CLUSTER ATTENDANCE

We have clear clusters highlighting a relationship breakdown and the entrance of another person into the dynamics. The cluster around the partner cards (Three of Swords, Ten of Pentacles, Two of Swords, Two of Wands, and Five of Pentacles) shows the breakdown of the marriage. Meanwhile, the Page of Swords, Three of Cups, Ace of Cups, and Two of Cups and the Lovers cluster to spotlight new love and a third party entering the situation.

In the significator square, we have three right-moving cards, which appear to walk backward into the past. This suggests that the querent has some issues to overcome from the past. With the Six of Swords heading backward into the Two of Wands, the querent needs to revisit some plans that need attention. Moreover, the King of Pentacles is surrounded by three right-facing cards, indicating a dynamic entrance. They are collectively moving toward the Queen of Cups, showing the incoming motion of the King of Pentacles.

Technique 5: Knights & Pages

Three knights are in attendance, showing that there will be a lot of development and action within the time frame, focusing on relationships (Knight of Cups), home/work (Knight of Pentacles), and conscious decisions (Knight of Swords). The directional cues of the Knights highlight two actions entering the querent's life (the Knight of Pentacles and Knight of Cups facing right) and one action taken by the querent (the Knight of Swords facing left).

KNIGHT OF PENTACLES

Start: Knight of Pentacles

Development: Seven of Pentacles, Ace of Cups

The action in the Knight of Pentacles relates to the King of Pentacles, who will soon enter the querent's life. This gentleman has struggled to get over a relationship, as indicated by the Seven of Pentacles, showing that the relationship was dying anyway, leading him to seek new love (Knight moving into Ace of Cups).

KNIGHT OF CUPS

Start: Knight of Cups

Development: Eight of Cups, Six of Cups

The action shown in the Knight of Cups also belongs to the King of Pentacles. In leaving a difficult relationship (Eight of Cups), he returns to the romantic he always was (movement to the Six of Cups).

PAGE OF SWORDS

Impact: Page of Swords

Source: Six of Cups, the Moon

The only Page in attendance (left facing), signifying chattiness and maybe even a little intelligent banter. The Page of Swords begins with the Moon, showing that the messages were undercover for a while, and they became very sentimental and happy in nature (note: this will be woven into your final interpretation).

Technique 6: The Direct Line of Sight

The direct line of sight of the querent shows the actual events within the querent's life. Inauspiciously, the Ten of Pentacles and Two of Swords indicate that her "happily ever after" is faltering (Ten of Pentacles inauspicious), and she is facing difficult decisions but is uncertain (Two of Swords inauspicious). She is heavily focused on the responsibilities she has accumulated within the relationship (Ten of Wands), but she will begin to see the light when she begins celebrating the breakup rather than considering it a burden (Three of Cups auspiciously following the Ten of Wands). Even though it feels too much (Ten of Wands), it is clear that the seeds have been sown for a new relationship (the Knight's action and flanking cards).

THE DIRECT LINE OF SIGHT: ADVANCED

In the Advanced Line of Sight, we incorporate the cards above and below the line of sight to explain further.

LINE OF SIGHT

Column 1:

After much arguing, the querent begins her year ahead with a painful split from her partner (Three of Swords in the direct line of sight, explained by the King of Cups, Ten of Cups, and Five of Swords inauspiciously).

Column 2:

She finds herself flummoxed by the aggressive and manipulative tactics employed by the King of Cups and knows she needs to plan for her future (Two of Swords explained by cards above and below).

Column 3:

She takes control of her life and contemplates the best way to move forward. The pain is still very real, and singledom has its downsides (Queen of Cups explained by cards above and below).

Column 4:

Whilst navigating her new direction, she realizes she has a lot more responsibilities (possibly even debts) that were previously undisclosed, but she is determined to forge forward (Ten of Wands explained by cards above and below).

Column 5:

Finally, she experiences a spark of joy at the breakup and the ultimate freedom it brings. The querent puts herself out there and begins to revel in being single (Three of Cups explained by the cards above and below; note that the Tower above the Three of Cups can refer to a reckless night out that is chaotic in nature but a whole heap of fun!).

Column 6:

Before long, the querent feels the first butterflies of a new relationship blossoming. A suitor enters, bringing all the amazing feelings of positivity. However, she is somewhat embarrassed about the reckless night on the town and maybe unsure of the image she projected of herself (the Ace of Cups explained by the cards above and below).

Column 7:

The new beau enters with full force as a possible suitor as opposed to a short date—a possible long-term companion. This leaves the querent wondering why he is so interested in her, but she enjoys it nonetheless! (Knight of Pentacles explained by the cards above and below).

Column 8:

There is always a temptation to find out what a new partner has not yet revealed—where they came from and what led to the disintegration of their previous relationship. The new partner struggles with his baggage, but the querent sees it as an opportunity to get to know one another on another level (Seven of Pentacles explained by cards above and below, read in conjunction with inauspicious meanings for the King of Pentacles and auspicious meanings for the querent).

Technique 7: The Cartomantic Approach

KNIGHTING

The Queen of Cups knights the following cards:

Inauspicious: Five of Swords / Three of Swords / the Magician

The querent has walked away from the crisis of the marriage and will acknowledge that they have caused pain by not being transparent.

Auspicious: The Tower / Knight of Swords / the Moon

Her strategy for leaving the relationship was to rip the Band-Aid off all at once and just disappear.

DIAGONALS

Negative dynamic influences: Two of Wands

The querent has no plans and is desperately seeking a way forward but lacks tangible plans.

Negative dynamic actions: Strength / King of Cups

There has been force inflicted on both sides—a stubborn standoff, or something more concerning?

Positive dynamic influence: Four of Swords

The querent should take a time out from the relationship to regroup their thoughts.

Positive dynamic action: Five of Pentacles / Page of Swords / Two of Cups

The querent must understand that they no longer have every resource available to them that was there before; it will feel like starting from scratch. However, the hardship will be worth it to find a new connection on the horizon.

MIRRORING

Any card can be chosen to mirror. I have highlighted the cards I would personally choose in this spread pertaining to the relationship.

Inauspicious:

- Ten of Cups (showing emotional ruin)
- King of Cups (the partner)
- Ten of Swords (showing troubled feelings beneath the Queen of Cups)
- Magician + Strength combo (to ensure the manipulation does not continue!)

TEN OF CUPS MIRRORS: Three of Swords (inauspicious) / Seven of Pentacles + Four of Wands (outcome)

The initial breakdown and heartache of the Ten of Cups begins the time frame, but by the end of the year, we can see that the querent will be working on regrowing her stability. It may be rocky at the beginning of the year but begins to flourish in the mirrored cards.

KING OF CUPS MIRRORS: Five of Swords (inauspicious) / Eight of Cups + the Devil

The partner is being sneaky and cannot be trusted, leading to his temptation to walk away.

TEN OF SWORDS MIRRORS: Queen of Cups / the Sun + Ace of Cups

The Queen of Cups will feel extreme pain at the breakup, but within six months we can see an incredible upturn and positive new experiences in love.

Auspicious:

- The Tower (what is the chaos and how does it present?)
- King of Pentacles (new beau)

THE TOWER MIRRORS: Page of Swords / Four of Swords + the Moon

The querent takes a timeout to delve deeply and consider everything that was wrong within the relationship. A little banter and messages incoming from the King of Pentacles start the chaos of the Tower in motion, and the querent finally breaks down and dissolves the life that she knew before.

KING OF PENTACLES MIRRORS: Knight of Pentacles / Strength + Two of Swords (inauspicious)

The querent is already manifesting her new love when she puts effort into reducing her confusion and making those difficult decisions. The ultimate decision to end her relationship opens the door for the King of Pentacles to enter.

Technique 8: The Master Method

The querent is seated in house 14 (Love), showing that she is in control of her love life and working very hard to rediscover the love she has for herself.

The partner (King of Cups) is seated in house 32 (Money), suggesting that his focus is only on the financial aspect of the relationship and nothing more.

The new suitor (King of Pentacles) is in house 18 (Pleasure)—this could show that he is a welcome enjoyment in her life. It suggests that he enjoys being part of her life, and also indicates that the relationship is more about pleasure than love within the set time frame.

The querent had lots of questions about their relationship. The following houses were chosen for closer inspection (note that the interpretations below include the auspicious versus inauspicious narrative):

HOUSE	ESSENCE
6. Wishes	Six of Swords; the querent would like to move on.
10. Loss	Knight of Pentacles; she will lose some of her financial income.
11. Trouble	Ace of Cups; the querent will struggle in matters of the heart.
12. State or Condition	Three of Cups; her situation is one that is worth celebrating!
13. Joy	Ten of Wands; the number of responsibilities will dampen her joy.
14. Love	Queen of Cups; she is in love or soon will be.
16. Marriage	Ten of Cups; her relationship is failing but she is currently still involved.

18. Pleasure	King of Pentacles; the new lover is a source of pleasure.
23. Lover	Strength (inauspicious), explaining that he is not currently a major force in her life.
27. Changes	Six of Cups; it's not so much about changing, rather returning to a happier state.
30. Misfortune/ Disgrace	Nine of Pentacles; financial independence will be extremely tough.
31. Happiness	The Magician; the querent struggles to create a happier world.
32. Money/Fortune	King of Cups; the partner is bothered only about finances and can also show the querent is dependent upon her partner for money.

In short, the querent is in control of her own love life; only she can make the decision to move on. She feels betrayed and knows that a split will cause financial problems, which will weigh heavily on her emotional decisions. She should remember that there will be a time to celebrate in the near future, and that she shouldn't allow the responsibilities of being financially independent dampen her enjoyment. Her relationship is breaking down, and her partner is interested only in how this financially affects him. There is a new suitor on the horizon who will bring a great deal of enjoyment, and she should remember that returning to a happier state of being is more important than any other change (or loss).

Technique 9: The Line of Fate

The intention for the line of fate is "This will NOT happen within the time frame."

Two of Cups + The Lovers + Six of Wands + Three of Wands

Whilst the querent is dissolving her current relationship and moving toward a new one, the new beau will not instantly become the love of her life, nor will they walk off majestically into the sunset within the set time frame. However, the fact that the love cards land in the line of fate shows that this development that is forthcoming will occur AFTER the set time frame. Therefore, this confirms that any relationship starting soon will have the opportunity to flourish into a deep and meaningful connection that will stand the test of time.

Technique 10: Timing

The tableau is set for eight months, with each column representing one month. The Queen of Cups faces left, indicating that our time frame begins with month 1 in the right-hand column.

Month 1:

The querent's marriage is breaking down (Ten of Cups), and the solid relationship she believed they had is interwoven with betrayal and ultimately heartache (Ten of Cups, Three of Swords, Five of Swords). It is a difficult month, showing that her partner is already ready to leave (King of Cups exiting).

Month 2:

The querent begins to plan and make important decisions about her relationship, but she struggles to think clearly (Two of Wands, Two of Swords). This is mainly due to the behavior of the partner, who is being extremely manipulative and assertive (the Magician, Strength).

Month 3:

The querent makes the break and keeps thinking of the new plans she is making (Six of Swords above her, traveling to the right to the Two of Wands). The separation is painful (Ten of Swords), and although she is happy, she is alone and the whole world is her oyster (Nine of Pentacles, Three of Wands). She is still grieving (Ten of Swords).

Month 4:

The querent begins to look at where this split leaves her as far as responsibilities are concerned (Ten of Wands), which requires her to step back from the situation and take a moment to consider (Four of Swords). She is worried about the unknown financial implications of this (Five of Pentacles, the Moon) and hasn't yet found how she can turn this around (Six of Wands in the line of fate).

Month 5:

After working through what responsibilities she has to take on after the split, she decides it is time to shake it up and go out on a binge party with girlfriends (Three of Cups following Ten of Wands), painting the town red (Knight of Swords action showing that she puts aside her hardships in the Five of Cups and moves into the Sun). In this moment of happiness with others, she begins chatting with another prospect (Page of Swords, Knight of Swords). This is not an instant connection (the Lovers in the line of fate), but it is one that could be in the future!

Month 6:

New emotions are brewing (Ace of Cups), but this also causes anxiety for the querent. Self-defeating thoughts such as "Why would he want me?" or "Will this end like the last?" enter (Nine of Swords), but they do not discourage the querent from experiencing the butterflies (Ace of Cups). The feelings remind the querent who she is and how much fun she had as a child—it is a feeling of "home" with the new gentleman.

Month 7:

The new gentleman is a major force in month 7; he takes over everything! Although it is exciting and fun, there is a slight concern from the querent that she cannot meet his expectations (the Devil next to the Four of Cups, showing that he is perhaps asking her to do something that she is not comfortable with).

Month 8:

The final month shows that the querent is really hoping that this relationship could be the right one for her and that it will grow. However, she should be careful not to jump in too quickly or be tempted to act irrationally in the first throes of love. Taking it a little slower will allow her to appreciate the solidity of the relationship before rushing into full-on marriage!

Client Readings

The Art of Reading a Tableau

When first looking at a tableau, it is easy to feel intimidated and almost fearful of the sheer number of cards and their meanings to digest and communicate. Before reading for others, begin by having fun with a tableau. Use them to tell stories about work, love, and random tales of kindness, sorrow, and life. Allow yourself to be immersed in the story, and to build not only a narrative but also a relationship with the tableaus themselves. Allow yourself to experience the rollercoaster of emotions as you flow through and really embrace the journey through the cards. Laugh, cry, and, above all else, tell the story the tableau shows you. This will build your confidence with tableaus and help you seamlessly knit together narratives with all their twists and turns. Think of it as watching, understanding, and narrating a portion of a life. Not only is this a great privilege, but also a great responsibility.

When you read for others, the stories you have practiced and gained confidence in will become the narrative of someone else's life, often during a time when they may not trust themselves or others. They will seek hope, clarity, and a sense of empowerment from the reading, which will give them the strength to face their current challenges and understand how best to move forward. This is the gift of accurate predictive reading.

We are blessed as readers to be able to delve into the lives of our querents and share both low points and high points alike. When laying a tableau, take a moment to consider your querent and the questions they bring to the table—inevitably numerous. Consider how fortunate you are to be honored with this insight during this very personal moment. As you begin to lay the cards, enjoy the moment and feel the core essence of each card as it falls into a house.

A tableau reading should flow seamlessly, without referencing card names or keywords, capturing the art of conversation within a Tarot reading. The techniques within this book will flow intuitively once you have practiced, and become second nature when forming your interpretations. Never force an interpretation; just allow the storyline to develop as you describe what you see in the cards.

My personal rule of thumb is to always seek substantiation for the interpretation I am completing. That is to say, if the cards suggest a marital breakdown, do the houses substantiate this? Can the use of knighting corroborate the evidence thus far? Do you have any clusters to confirm? Every technique contained herein will allow you to double-check your interpretation over and over again, leaving no doubt as to the validity of your predictions. Moreover, are the cards around the partner card confirming their pain and suffering in the situation? Substantiation is the key to predictive accuracy.

How I Read for Clients:

Each client has their own experiences in life—we must always appreciate that they come to the table with trials and tribulations that we may not have experienced ourselves. I always begin a reading by thanking the querent and asking what has guided them to me. It is a simple and short exchange where we, as readers, can gauge the current status of their situation and how to best lead the reading. As a professional reader, we must always control the flow of the reading to ensure that our clients walk away with the best reading possible. A client is often emotional and not in the clearest state of mind when they purchase a reading. It is important to listen carefully and take notes if needed to understand what the querent is actually asking.

For example, a client may ask for a relationship reading. After listening to their opening remarks, the reader deciphers what they really want to find out. A relationship reading could range from "Will I meet the partner of my dreams?" to "Is my partner faithful?" Only by listening to the querent can we understand the pertinent questions to ask or seek answers to. One question often leads to many more when we think logically; for example, "Is my partner faithful?" can lead to "Would it be in my best interest to remain in this relationship?" Make notes as you listen to your querent and consider what you would ask in that situation.

In a typical hour-long session, I will lay three to four Grand Tableaus, such as the following:

- A general predictive overview of the situation in the year ahead

- A themed Grand Tableau including work/love/finances/health, etc.

- Advice for the querent about how to best overcome any obstacles

- A "What will happen in the time frame if the querent takes the advice from the last spread?" tableau

The above are interchangeable on the basis of the querent's questions, and at each juncture I discuss with the client what we have learned and what further inspection is needed, ensuring that they leave the session with no unanswered questions.

After the initial exchange, I advise my querent that I will be silent for a moment as I lay the cards. This sets the expectations and flow of the reading. Whilst laying a tableau, I count the houses in my head (for example, the Two of Wands is in house 1: Projects, and the Empress is in house 2: Satisfaction). This process helps form associations between the cards and houses while considering the theme of the reading. It allows time to process each card within its placement and begin interpreting the storyline in my mind. I also look at attendance and whether the suits, Majors, or numbers are clustering to confirm the direction of the read.

Once all cards are laid out, I begin interpreting, bringing the information learned whilst considering the cards into the overall context of the storyline. I explain what the significator placement means for the year ahead and how the Court cards interact to describe interpersonal relationships. Next, I move into the significator square to confirm the status of the querent within the situation shown.

I complete the significator square for any people of interest within the spread and then move into the direct line of sight, incorporating the cards above and below into the free-flow narrative of the line of sight—technically, by this stage I have read every card within the tableau! I also use the houses continually to substantiate the storyline, adding cartomantic techniques (knighting, diagonals, and mirroring) to delve into the juicy influences and backstories. I also always check the line of fate to see what situation is revealed as out of control in the set time frame, since it is a great indicator of whether the querent will or will not have the outcome they are hoping for in the year ahead.

Once the core essence of the situation(s) is shown, it is normal for further questions to arise. It is good practice to frequently check in with the client to ensure that all their questions are being answered, especially if the cards highlight troublesome times ahead.

Aiding a querent through challenging life events is an important part of our role, and it is essential that we deliver a difficult reading with compassion. We mustn't put a positive spin on negative cards, for we are not serving our clients well if they are not forewarned of difficulties. However, we do need to understand the impact of our words. Beware of using harsh keywords and consider how you would communicate with a friend in need. We cannot erase the difficulties to come by ignoring a negative card, but we can offer the news in a compassionate manner.

The language of a storyteller is the perfect narrative flow. Make sure your readings are conversational in nature and not stunted with card keywords. Imagine that you are sitting with a friend, drinking coffee and chatting about the world's news—this is the perfect form of narrative language for a tableau reading.

Our most important role as a reader is often that of a coach and advisor, guiding the querent on how to navigate the situation for the best possible outcome. An advice spread at the end of every reading on "how to get the most out of the time frame" is a wonderful way to empower the querent moving forward, providing clear and concise steps about what action they can take to overcome any issue.

Most importantly, take your role as reader seriously and with pride, but don't forget to enjoy your cards and have fun interpreting the story of life!

Additional Resources

If you would like to learn more about the Tarot tableau or wish to add a new divination system to your belt, you will find everything you need here:

World Divination Association: www.worlddivinationassociation.com

The Card Geek YouTube: www.youtube.com/c/thecardgeek

Untold Tarot: The Lost Art of Reading Ancient Tarot by Caitlín Matthews (REDFeather).

About the Author

TONI SAVORY (formerly Puhle) was born in Sheffield in 1975. As a child she would speak with spirit and learned at an early age how to share divination with those around her. Toni has studied and researched the traditional systems of Tarot, Lenormand, Kipper, and Gypsy cards in England, France, Germany, and Austria. She lived a stone's throw from Munich, where the first Kipper deck originated, and not far from the roots of the Game of Hope in Nuremberg. The last 15 years have been devoted to researching divination in Bavaria, meeting amazing generational readers and families who passed down the art of reading.

Toni is founder of the World Divination Association and author of *The Card Geek's Guide to Kipper Cards*, *Rainbow Kipper*, *Lustrous Lenormand* companion book, and the *World Divination Association Palmistry & Skat Manuals*. Her degrees in French and German have opened up source material for the systems she teaches and have given her a unique understanding of the decks in a range of European settings.

Toni's YouTube Channel contains hundreds of "how to" videos, and she teaches a variety of courses on traditional divination systems, face to face or through the World Divination Association.

Toni is now living in the heart of Northern Ireland with her two boys and her partner, Jane Matthews.